CHERISH THE EARTH

CHERISH THE EARTH

Mary Low

WILD GOOSE PUBLICATIONS
www.ionabooks.com

Acknowledgements

Thanks to the following copyright holders for permission to reproduce prayers, poems or prose items in this anthology. Every effort has been made to trace copyright holders, but we would be glad to hear from anyone whom we have been unable to contact. Further copyright details for contributions are given on pages 201–216.

To John Agard c/o Caroline Sheldon Literary Agency for 'Rainbow' from his book *Limbo Dancer in Dark Glasses*; Meg Bateman for 'Ealghol: Dà Shealladh'; Birlinn Ltd for the extract from *Red Rowans and Wild Honey* by Betsy White; David Bolt Associates for 'Beware Soul Brother' by Chinua Achebe; Eunice Buchanan for 'The Hornie Gollach'; Carcanet Press for 'The Bonnie Broukit Bairn' by Hugh MacDiarmid; Catholic Truth Society and Wm. B. Eerdmans Publishing Co. for the extract from *Sollicitudo Rei Socialis* by Pope John Paul II; Taing gu Aonghas Pàdraig Caimbeul airson 'Ag Iasgach a' Mhic-Meanmna'. the Church of England Archbishops' Council for the extracts from *Common Worship: Services and Prayers for the Church of England* and *The Alternative Service Book, 1980*. Further thanks to: the Church of Scotland Panel on Worship for 'Creator God'; Inus Daneel for two prayers from the Association of African Earth-keeping Churches; the Mrs H.M. Davies Will Trust for 'A Child's Pet' by W.H.Davies; Oliver Davies for his translations 'Glorious Lord', 'Antiphon to the Holy Spirit' by Hildegard of Bingen, and the extract from the Life of Melangell; Éditions du Cloître for 'Prière d'un Chien' by Carmen Bernos de Gasztold; Faber and Faber Ltd for 'A Disaster' by Ted Hughes and for 'Faith in a Seed' by Barbara Kingsolver; Fortress Press and Sallie McFague for the extract from *Super, Natural Christians*; Gomer Press for 'Reredos' by Euros Bowen and 'The Ancient Wood' by Waldo Williams translated by Tony Conran; Harcourt for the extract from Thomas Merton's *The Sign of Jonas*;

HarperCollins Australia for 'Night Herons' by Judith Wright from her *Collected Poems*; Sue Ellen Herne for 'Mohawk Prayer'; Brent Hodgson for 'The Voice of God'; Satish Kumar for his 'Thought for the Day'; Michael Leunig for 'We give thanks' and 'God help us to change'. 'Bean an Iasgair' and 'Casan Sioda' are reproduced by permission of the Lorimer Trust and Estate of George Campbell Hay. Thanks to Eric Lott for 'Bread Prayer'; Fearghus MacFhionnlaigh for the extract from 'Iolair, Brù-Dhearg, Giuthas' and to Ronald Black for his translation; Hugh Montefiore for the extract from the Church of England *Man and Nature* report; Ivo Moseley for his translation of 'Yes to the Earth' by Sibilla Aleramo; Breandán Ó Madagáin for 'Creativity'; Mary Oliver and Beacon Press, Boston for 'The Summer Day' from her book *House of Light*; Orbis Books for the extract from *Cry of the Earth, Cry of the Poor* by Leonardo Boff; Ruth Page for the extract from her *The Web of Creation*; PaterNoster Publishing and Wm. B. Eerdmans Publishing Co. for the extract from Calvin's *Commentaries*; Pax Christi for the extract from *Be Still and Know* by Thich Nat Hanh; Penguin Books for the extracts from Augustine's *City of God* and the adaptation from *The Brothers Karamazov* by Fyodor Dostoyevsky; Jonathon Porritt for the extract from 'Let the Green Spirit Live'; Chaim and Adena Potok and Random House, Inc. for the extract from *The Book of Lights* by Chaim Potok; The Random House Group Ltd for 'The Light Trap' by John Burnside, published by Jonathan Cape; Kathleen Raine for 'Word Made Flesh' and 'Disconnected Souls'. Thanks to Schroder Music Co. for the words of 'God Bless the Grass'; Rhena Schweitzer Miller for the extract from Albert Schweitzer's *Civilisation and Ethics;* HarperCollins New York for the extract from *Reverence for Life* by Albert Schweitzer; Hamid Shami for 'Lost'; Alan Spence for 'Today'; Kenneth Steven and Saint Andrew Press for 'The Changes'; SPCK for the prayer of absolution from an RSPCA service by Andrew Linzey and for items collected and edited by John Carden; Dorcas

Symms for 'Barley Field'; Gwydion Thomas for 'The Other' and 'The Coming' by R.S. Thomas; Derick Thomson for 'Urnaigh Iain Ruaidh'; Oxford University Press for Robert W. Thomson's translation of Athanasius. Thanks also to Carol Watson for 'Traffic', 'War', 'Animals', and 'Sorry'; to Mainstream Publishing for the extract from Kenneth White's 'The Bird Path'; Wesleyan University Press for 'The Heaven of Animals' by James Dickey; The World Council of Churches for 'Lord of Lords, Creator of all things' ('West African Harvest Thanksgiving'); WWF-UK for the extract from 'Science within Islam' by Yunus Negus;

The majority of biblical quotations are from *The New Revised Standard Version of the Bible*, copyright © 1989 by the Division of Christian Education of the National Council of Churches of Christ in the USA. Used by permission. All rights reserved.

Other biblical quotations are from *The Good News Bible* published by The Bible Societies/HarperCollins Publishers Ltd. UK © American Bible Society, 1966, 1971, 1976, 1992. Used by permission.

To Mhairi and Eilidh
One Day

CONTENTS

FOREWORD

Making worshippers of us

It used to be in Scotland that every child was expected to know the Shorter Catechism by heart, and to be able to answer the question, *'What is man's chief end?'* with the words, *'Man's chief end is to glorify God.'* As people of faith, we are called above all to celebrate God. But 'God' is an abstract concept. So we celebrate what we see, God revealed in the creation; we celebrate what we trust, God-with-us in Jesus; we celebrate what we experience, God's Spirit moving among people, reconciling and liberating; we celebrate what we hope for, God's commonwealth of justice and love. And beyond all these, we celebrate the mystery of grace and generosity at the heart of life.

The instinct to worship in response to the beauty and mystery of the universe is as old as the human story itself. The passionate outpouring of the Psalmist in Psalm 104 is a song of praise to God the Creator which echoes down the centuries and still resonates today in the hearts of everyone who has ever looked out over mountain ranges folded into blue mist, or at innumerable stars over the desert, or out across a sparkling sea and wondered. That song of praise for the intricate delicacy of a leaf unfurling, for the massive solidity of granite and basalt, for the corn high in the field and the horse racing across a meadow has moved humankind to express its love for the earth our home in a thousand ways.

In the late Middle Ages, the poets and singers of Scotland were known as 'Makars', makers. It is not too fanciful to imagine the universe as the song of God the Makar, a joyous outpouring of energy and creativity and wild ordering and continuous exchange. And it is truly a religious instinct to respond to God's song-making with our antiphon of praise. Creation makes worshippers of us.

Almighty God, Creator:
The morning is yours, rising into fullness.
The summer is yours, dipping into autumn.
Eternity is yours, dipping into time.
The vibrant grasses, the scent of flowers, the lichen on the rocks,
*   the tang of seaweed,*
All are yours.
Gladly we live in this garden of your creating.

In Genesis 2, we find a wonderful picture of God the Makar. There is something rather touching, both literally and emotionally, about this God, so profoundly human in his activity – modelling a man out of the earth's clay, animating (literally, breathing life into) him, then planting a beautiful garden full of magical trees and treasure for him to live in. But the man himself is as much a part of the earth as all the other forms and species. His very name, Adam, links him with the ground (Adamah) of his being. He is created, not creator.

The failure to acknowledge createdness has been a big problem for human beings ever since – and an even bigger one for the other life forms we share the earth with. Our tendency to assume that the universe is at our disposal, that it has no intrinsic worth other than its utility to the human species has made us careless to the point of extreme culpability. In the last twenty-five years alone, we have destroyed 30% of our non-renewable natural environment. It is a kind of blasphemy. How can we pray to God the Creator with integrity when we are so cavalier with God's creation?

Always in the beauty, the foreshadowing of decay.
Nature red and scarred as well as lush and green.
In the garden also, always the thorn …

To be creature, one among many, is to come face to face with our limitations. We are not God, and God is not just an idealised version of us. God is other, and speaks to us in other voices. Our judgement of the world, sometimes expressed as if we had a monopoly on divine truth, is in truth that which holds us most to account. In Micah 6, the prophet calls the people as if to a court of law to listen to what God is saying, and this is what God the plaintiff says: *Arise, plead your case before the mountains, and let the hills hear your voice. Hear, you mountains, the controversy of the Lord, and you enduring foundations of the earth; For the Lord has a controversy with his people, and he will contend with Israel.* There can be no clearer indication anywhere in Scripture that to be creature in the covenant is not only to be required to be in right relationship with our own human kind, but with the whole creation. Justice is also eco-justice. And how, then, will the mountains judge us? Will the enduring foundations of the earth find in our favour?

In Job 38, the voice of God challenges human egotism: … *Have you comprehended the vast expanse of the world? … doubtless you know, for you were already born. So long is the span of your life!* This God is scary! Who would not, like Job, crumple in humiliation, silenced by such withering sarcasm. The tone reminds me a little of my daughter at fifteen: 'Oh Mum, you don't know *anything!*' I remember as I grew to adulthood, being amazed at how much my mother had learned! It is one of the most painful lessons of adulthood, realising how little we really know, and how much less we can command. The struggle to impose our will on everything around us, including the earth, causes grave damage to the environment, to other people and to ourselves.

The Iona Community has since its inception been committed to justice for and the wellbeing of people living in poverty. Increasingly people concerned with human justice and those concerned with eco-justice have seen how greatly these two are interconnected and interdependent. Mary Low's anthology, and especially her introduction, remind us that when one part of the body suffers, all the other parts suffer with it, including the earth's body.

Job was called to let God be God. Even with all our scientific insight, what we know about the universe is so much less than what is still mysterious to us. The created order in all its complexity and beauty moved a quantum physicist to say that the appropriate response to it is one of sheer wonder and love. But such a celebration requires the dethronement of human ego, and the birth of co-operation with nature rather than domination over it.

Lord, by the glories of your creation, which we did not devise,
fan our faith to flame.

Celebration involves carefulness. And we take care of what we value. The word 'cherish' derives from the Latin *carus*, meaning 'dear' or 'precious'. To cherish is to hold dear, to set a high value on, to care for. From the same root come both 'charity' and 'caress'. In the old marriage service of the Church of Scotland, husband and wife both promised to love, honour and *cherish* (not obey!). This is a tender and intimate word, and its use in the title of this book invites us to a re-evaluation of our relationship with the earth. It is in the nature of human beings to be in *dialogue*, to ask a question, to start a conversation, to yearn for communication.

But communication begins with attentiveness. In the close and patient observation of creatures in the wild, of plants and minerals, of seas and rivers, which so many of the contributions to this anthology demonstrate, human beings discover something about the nature of them, their particularities, their strengths; the ways in which our createdness is similar and yet different. As someone who has experienced the 'geo-poetics' of Kenneth White with the force of revelation, I am quite convinced that poetry, prose and prayer can help this re-evaluation. I love the great prayer of George MacLeod's quoted in this foreword. It prays the mystery of the cosmic Christ, a mystery I cannot grasp hold of by analysis but which encompasses me in poetry. This created universe is alive with a life I participate in, and in my participation I am in Christ.

In You, all things consist and hang together.

The life of our participation in Christ is resurrection life. In Christ, the whole created order is raised. God, being earthed, raises earth to heaven. We are encompassed by the stuff of eternity. Such stuff demands respect. Jesus embodied the potential of life lived in solidarity with the purposes of God's realm. All that degrades or denies that potential is a kind of blasphemy, all that cherishes and affirms it is praise. So let us cherish the earth.

Holy Spirit, Enlivener,
in this new creation, already upon us,
fill us with life anew.

—Kathy Galloway

Introduction

'FROM A DISTANCE, the earth looks blue and green, and the snow-capped mountains white.' It seems no time since this was one of the songs of the moment, but apparently the earth does not look as green as it used to. I heard this over the breakfast table one morning, courtesy of the BBC. The interviewer was speaking to one of the crew on board the International Space Station and the line fizzed and beeped as they chatted amiably about food and weightlessness and, inevitably, the view. We could all picture it, our jewel of a planet in an ink-black sky. He was talking about weather. They could see storms and droughts, he said. At night they saw cities: 'It's quite amazing how many people actually live down there and how much effect they are having on the environment.' Suddenly, it was as if he had remembered something he really wanted to say. Things had changed, he announced, since his first flight in 1990: 'I have seen changes in what comes out of some of the rivers, and in land usage. We see areas of the world that are being burned to clear land, so we are losing lots of trees. There is smoke and dust in wider-spread areas than we have seen before, particularly as areas of

Africa dry up in certain regions. We have to be very careful how we treat this good Earth we live on.'[i]

Less than a fortnight later, violence erupted in the United States, Israel and Afghanistan and 'this good earth' slipped down the international agenda yet again. How do you keep your mind on a long-term problem when every day brings more immediate ones? Unless you are one of the millions of people who already live in a badly degraded environment, it is easy to feel remote from the issue, enjoying the fruits and the beauty of the earth while at the same time contributing to its problems.[ii]

Maybe the truth is that we cannot and will not change. Perhaps the disaster envisaged by Ted Hughes (p.63) is already under way. At the time of writing, it has proved impossible to get all the governments in the world to agree to the small reduction in greenhouse gas emissions which might, just might, slow down the present rate of climate change by the year 2050. Perhaps, as my auntie says, we will 'invent something' but in the meantime change depends on political will, and this is in turn supposed to depend on the will of the people. What we want, our desires, are central to the problem – and also to the solution. For years, organisations like Greenpeace and Friends of the Earth have been urging us to make changes in our lifestyle. They have not always been popular or one hundred per cent right, but their high-profile campaigns have kept the issues in the public eye, to the point where governments are beginning, very slowly, to take action. Some have set targets for renewable energy and are looking at alternative transport systems, water conservation and other measures. Others seem locked into destructive policies, determined to gobble up resources for as long as possible in the name of national interest, though in the long term even this requires change. For people of faith, there is another dimension to all this. What we do to our environment, and to other creatures, is influenced, for better or for worse, by what we believe about God's way for the world and its human and non-human inhabitants.

I get some revealing responses when I tell people that I am interested in beliefs about nature. 'Oh, you mean druids?' said a famous journalist from the Western Isles. A woman from Greenpeace found it difficult to understand why anyone should be interested in the Kyoto Protocol *and* Christianity. A local justice and peace organisation told me, with obvious regret, that they had recently had to cancel a one-day conference on the environment due to lack of interest. Perhaps, they suggested, green Christianity was 'still a bit rarefied for Scotland'. When I mentioned eco-theology to a farming friend, he was appalled. 'Dear God,' he said, 'can they not leave anything alone?' It's possible that he meant ecologists, but I'm pretty sure he meant theologians. He has little time for either, and does not usually expect religious professionals to have any understanding of his situation, or any area of competence outside the pulpit. In all of this, the perception seems to be that Christianity has little or nothing to say about the relationship between God, humans and the non-human natural world; and that when it does try to speak, it has little grasp of the realities of the situation.

Christians might respond that this is a new subject and that we have simply not had time to come to grips with it. There is an element of truth in this. Ecology is a relatively new subject for everyone, but the churches do seem to have been particularly slow to take an interest in it at parish level. It is as if we simply do not see it as part of our tradition. But, of course, it is. Ecotheology may be a new discipline, born of the present crisis, but there have always been people who wondered how the *oikia* (household, family) of nature related to the *oikia* of God, and what this might mean for human behaviour. It is one of the oldest questions in the book. It is there in primal religions and was too important to be dropped when people moved on to other more universal faiths. This is why Canaan-ite festivals underlie Judaic ones and pre-Christian festivals underlie

Christian ones all over Europe: because life and fertility were understood to be given by a power or powers beyond ourselves, and while faith in that power remained, people wanted to work with it, rather than against it. At the same time, Christians have been keen to distance themselves from 'paganism'. Some have even attempted to cut themselves off from nature altogether, as from a seductress or a wicked uncle. This kind of spiritual escapology has never attracted much of a following, but it has certainly had an influence. Even allowing for the more earthy, compassionate Christianity which pre-dates it, it seems that for much of our history Christians have been so busy thinking about heaven that we have become like the dancers in Chinua Achebe's perceptive poem (p.118) 'Beware Soul Brother', levitating skywards and abandoning the earth to 'the long ravenous tooth' of self-interest and voracious consumerism.

There is no obvious support for this in the Gospels. True, there are apocalyptic passages in which worldly action of any kind seems futile, and there are glimpses of another world, and a desire to go there.[iii] But the Hebrew Bible views creation as a community of creatures before God; the Law and the prophets are about living fairly and happily in this world; and Jesus associates himself with both of these traditions, as we shall see. I grew up with the Bible. We read it Sunday by Sunday and sang about the wonders of creation, but it was never much more than a backdrop to the drama of salvation. Not that we were alone in this. I do not remember even hearing the word 'environment' till about 1970, though ecology had arrived as a science by 1953.[iv] By the end of primary school, however, we knew about animal extinctions. A group of us once clubbed together to buy Armand Dennis's *Animal* magazine, mainly for the picture of a lynx on the front cover, but what we found inside was a feature about Rachel Carson's recently published *Silent Spring*.[v] I struggled to understand it, but it left an enduring mark on my childhood consciousness.

Making this anthology has been a learning experience for me: getting to know the literature, speaking to theorists and to people who live and work with non-human nature from day to day. It has been impossible to do this without reflecting on my own attitudes to nature and my own unfinished journey towards ecological awareness, and perhaps that is what I can most usefully share with the reader at this point, since I am not an ecotheologian by trade. Some introductions simply describe what is to come in a book. This keeps the subject safely at arm's length and allows the editor to remain anonymous and uninvolved. But there is no one who is uninvolved with nature. As Kathleen Raine says, 'we ourselves are part of the earth we know' (p123) and if we are serious about cherishing it, then each of us needs to begin exploring our own relationship with it, not just as an intellectual exercise but as something which impinges on our everyday lives. We need to think about it collectively as well as individually (p.123), but I have decided to follow the example of many good women before me and 'get personal' since, in the words of Kathy Galloway, 'the political only becomes real ... when it is grounded in the personal' and the same can be said about religion.[vi] Below, then, you will find three memories each followed by a short reflection. I am not trying to set myself up as spokesperson for a very diverse group of people. I am simply trying to recapture how it seemed to me at the time. Some of the details are imaginary, but not the basic outlines. My hope is that this will evoke answering or contrasting memories in others, so that we can begin to bring this supposedly 'rarefied' subject down to earth.

* * *

Sunday morning in Edinburgh, May 1959. A young woman gets her two small children up and dressed. 'We're not going to church today,' she says. The children can hardly believe their luck. The girl knows better than to show her delight. The boy starts doing somersaults on the rug. 'Just this once,' says his mother firmly, 'and only because your father is away and I'm not taking the two of you to church on my own.'

They walk through deserted streets and catch a bus to the Hermitage, a little glen on the south side of the city. She shows them where birds are nesting, lifts them up to see – 'Sssh. Don't frighten her' – and where first they saw only darkness and a mess of twigs, now they see a sharp little eye watching them, and the smooth brown feathers of a hen-blackbird. They throw sticks from a bridge into a burn, then sit on a bench and drink orange juice and eat digestive biscuits. More than forty years later, the memory of it is still sweeter on my tongue than honey.

It was a long time before church held any kind of appeal for the little girl that I was then. The fustiness of it, the wordiness of it, were deadening experiences for a child. Nowadays we have children's liturgies and family services, but not then. Looking back, though, I have come to believe that if God is anywhere present in this world, 'he' was present for us there that morning. Why is this so hard for me to say? Even now, my finger hovers over the delete button, as if there were some terrible danger in admitting that God might reveal himself in the world of nature, on a Sunday morning, outside the church. To non-churchgoers, this discomfort might seem strange, even ridiculous; others, inside and outside the church, might think I am promoting 'paganism' or going soft in the head. For my own part, I am afraid of betraying something important.

Those of us who feel like this are part of a tradition. One of our spiritual ancestors would be Elijah (p.103) who found God not in the earthquake, wind or fire or in any of the powers of nature which his neighbours held sacred, but in something quiet and indefinable which followed: 'sheer silence' or 'a still small voice'. Another would be Augustine of Hippo who sat one day looking out over the African landscape, then turned away and wrote this: 'The eyes delight in the beautiful shapes of different sorts and bright attractive colours. I would not have these things take possession of my soul. Let God possess it, he who made them all. He made them all *very good*, but it is he who is my Good, not they.' *vii*

Augustine did not hate nature. On the contrary, he loved it so much that it frightened him. He was afraid that he would lose himself in it and be ruled by it. God and nature were always rivals for Augustine. He could appreciate it as God's creation, following Genesis (p.95) and the Psalmist (p.51) but it was always a distraction for him. Towards the end of his life, he allowed himself one long meditation on its loveliness (p.91) but the way to God was always elsewhere for him, in the inner world of thoughts and feelings and, above all, in the sacraments of the Church.

Whatever else might be said about this view of things, it has helped to create strong communities of faith around the teachings of Jesus of Nazareth and the various understandings of his life. There have been moments of glory and moments of infamy, as with all human institutions, but I have yet to find a better rule of life than 'love God and your neighbour as yourself', especially when combined with a belief in a loving, forgiving God with an inside knowledge of life on earth. Where else can we be challenged *and* comforted like this? We would probably find some equivalent in other religions, or humming away quietly in the hearts and minds of people who never go to church. But I still find it most easily in my own tradition with its regular pattern of Sunday celebration. I love walking in the country and I can understand why people say the whole earth is a temple or a mosque (p.54) and that forests are like cathedrals. I agree with all that. But I can also understand why Augustine thought there was something above and beyond the world of nature. And that is what I would not want to betray.

But could it not be that God comes to us in and through nature *as well as* through scripture and tradition? And since these could not exist for us outside of our own human nature, then nature is the condition of all our human words and ideas and also the condition of faith. My childhood experience was not yet about words and ideas. It was about my mother and brother, a blackbird, and the flavour of orange juice; but because it took place on a Sunday morning, in what I already thought of (with no great enthusiasm) as God's time, God and nature came together in my experience in a way which I could never forget.

Of course, there were many things I did not yet understand – good things about Christianity, ugly things about nature – but perhaps I knew something that morning which sermons and Sunday schools would gradually push to the back of my mind. When the fourth evangelist wrote that 'the Word was made flesh and dwelt among us' (p.106) he did not mean any disrespect to God; nor did he mean that God only became present for us spiritually in a special building. He meant, surely, that God became fully part of this world and lived in it as a human being, in holy places sometimes, but more often in unholy and quite ordinary ones, as well as in the midst of nature.

This was not an entirely new idea. In the Hebrew Bible, God does not just create the world. He also visits it, rests his feet on it, breathes life into it. Then in the New Testament, this presence crystallises into flesh and blood, molecules and atoms, in the person of Jesus.[viii] And he doesn't just borrow the stuff for a while, then shrug it off afterwards like an old coat. He transforms it and takes it with him into glory. Such was the understanding which gradually took shape among the first followers of Jesus, as they struggled to make sense of his violent death and their own experiences in the weeks which followed. A whole theology developed from this, mostly in terms of what it meant for human beings, but some early Christians, notably St Paul, believed that it gave hope to the whole of creation (p.110) and we see an imaginative flowering of this idea in the Irish apocryphal text *The Evernew Tongue* (p.111).

This view of reality, this coming together of divine holiness with messy material existence, did not come easily to everyone in the Mediterranean world. Theologians like Athanasius (p.107) had to struggle to convince people that God could be intimate with nature – 'present in all things ... containing and enclosing them in himself' – without compromising his transcendent otherness. Leontius (p.54) had to explain that he was not worshipping nature, but God *through* nature and the argument has continued down the centuries. As the ecological crisis gives it new impetus, there is particular interest in St Paul's belief (p.111) that we live and move and have our being in God. It is central to Teilhard's vision of *le milieu divin* – the God-pervaded universe [ix] – and its influence continues in writers like Sallie McFague: 'To say that God is always present is simply to acknowledge that God is reality, the breath, the life, the power, the love beneath, above, around, and in everything. This is the divine transcendence *immanently* experienced: it is the magnificence and awesomeness of God *with us*.'[x] Of course, there is still a danger of getting lost in the natural world around us, just as we can get lost in the (equally natural) inner worlds of thought and emotion, but incarnational theology can help us to see nature as leading towards, rather than away from, God. So those of us who still have occasional or even serious misgivings about nature can begin to look at it a little less warily.

I say *a little less* because as soon as we move beyond childhood innocence and romantic feelings about nature, we find cruelty as well as beauty, indifference as well as love. This is the experience of Albert Schweitzer (p132), George Campbell Hay (pp.128/29) and Sibilla Aleramo (p.134) and it raises some of the most painful and real questions about nature that it is possible to ask. But can we really talk about the 'cruelty' of a bacterium, or the 'indifference' of a beautiful landscape? And if not, where does this apparent cruelty come from? From God? From some chronic disorder of the universe? I do not pretend to have the answers, but if Jesus shows us what God is like, then God is surely the enemy of cruelty and indifference. This does not stop nature from seeming or being cruel, but for most of us, most of the time, the more urgent question is: can we do anything about it?

* * *

My second memory is very different from the first. In fact, it makes me cringe. February 1972 and I am a student volunteer in a youth club in the basement of an Edinburgh church. It's a Friday night and I am on the door, backed up by Malkie, an enormous vet student who can quell troublemakers simply by standing up straight. The band is taking a break, but we can see back into the hall. Someone has got up on stage. 'Hello,' he says, tapping the microphone, 'I'm from Friends of the Earth.'

There is a momentary dip in the noise-level as people turn to look at him, a slight boy with a kind of resolute innocence about him. The hum of conversation begins again. One of the other organisers shambles towards us: 'Who is this prat?' he asks. We shrug. I scan the room for someone who might know, but we all look equally bemused. Students from various churches and backgrounds, we know each other well, and I can overhear some comments and imagine others: Half the world is starving and we're supposed to worry about trees? What about the miners' strike, capitalism, the bomb? And from the evangelicals among us: what's this got to do with saving souls? A drinks can flies through the air. Malkie doesn't move. The crowd begin to heckle in a desultory kind of way. It's Friday night, for goodness' sake. We're supposed to be having fun.

I remember feeling sorry for the young man and being surprised at the vehemence of the response, but I didn't say anything. Many things seemed more important than trees and birds, not least the success of our Friday night. What I had failed to see – what we all failed to see – was any connection between what we thought we believed in, and our attitude towards the rest of creation. Why were we so angry with him? Perhaps because we realised that taking him seriously would make demands on us. I remember that sinking feeling: not another thing to worry about, on top of exams, relationships and the state of the (human) world. Surely nature could look after itself. So there was denial and, at the same time, a genuine concern about other things.

For a start, I agreed with the objection: 'Half the world is starving and we're supposed to worry about trees?' Those of us who felt like this were in touch with an old, entirely realistic fear that non-human nature might do harm to people: that there might be too much rain or not enough; that there might be rats or blight or epidemics. Many of the prayers in this book arise from exactly this fear: the prayer for rain (p.150), the harvest thanksgiving (p.89). It is a fear which needs to be addressed. It is not foolish. In the early seventies, young people like us were more likely to be aware of the risks to humans from non-human nature than of any threat posed by us to it.

Secondly, we were more concerned about human nature and the conflicts and cruelties within us. We knew that many natural disasters are caused or exacerbated by war or the ill-treatment of one people by another. So we confessed our complicity in the world's ills, went on marches, signed petitions. Many of us had a sense of being part of a big international family, regardless of race or creed (gender was still to come) and we wanted to be peacemakers or, if necessary, troublemakers for the kingdom of God. Not that we had a wildly optimistic view of ourselves. On the contrary, some of us developed an unhealthy preoccupation with sin. But the same tradition which gave us this also gave us an assurance of being loved by God, and the basics of a spirituality. So we were not unconcerned about nature. But it was all our own.

Also, we wanted to have fun and to be accepted within our own small circle of acquaintances. For all the earnestness of our fellowship meetings (which not all of us attended) we were no different from young people anywhere else. One afternoon it snowed and a whole crowd of us skipped lectures to go up into the Braid Hills and roll around in it. Nature was our playground that day. We did not believe that it was threatened, nor did we see ourselves as being part of it, though our bodies pursued their own agenda, secretly, like the sly young animals that we were.

There was a mixture of insight and ignorance in all this. We did not know, for example, that parts of the scientific community blamed Christianity for the environmental crisis;[xi] nor did we know that the Church of England was already preparing a report on the subject (p.143), following on the heels of William Temple (p.122) and Ralph Inge (p.62) decades before. Care for the earth had also begun to find its way into Catholic social teaching[xii] and Rosemary Ruether was about to start work on her early eco-feminist theology, *New Woman, New Earth*. The slow trickle of official documents which began in the 1970s, gathered momentum in the 80s and 90s with parallel developments in theology, and when the Church of Scotland report *While the Earth Endures* (p.175) appeared in 1986, it sold out in two editions. I was involved in other things by then and paid little attention, though I did notice that people involved with the World Council of Churches had begun talking about justice, peace *and the integrity of creation*.[xiii] I liked the sound of this, but doubted whether it was possible to support both environmental issues and issues of justice and peace.

We had not yet heard of liberation theology with its practical emphasis and its engagement with social realities, but we were its natural allies, children of the social gospel movement which had been around in Scotland for many years. When I did eventually hear about people like Gustavo Guttierez and Leonardo Boff, I admired them, alongside the mystics and philosophers who had captivated me earlier. I did not see that they would eventually have to come to terms with the environmental crisis, just as they had to come to terms with feminism. So when Boff began linking liberation theology with ecology in the mid-90s, I did not know whether to be excited or dismayed. Had this stalwart of the poor south finally gone soggy, or had he found a way to link two things which I had thought were irreconcilable? The latter was closer to the mark. He was not the first in the field by a long way, but he had finally realised the extent of the problem. The task of thinking about everyone and everything all together began to look inescapable.*xiv*

The arguments for a green liberation theology usually go something like this: God's way for the world, as proclaimed by Jesus, is good news for the poor. Loving your neighbour as yourself involves caring about how people live here and now. There is no other planet and our present rate of using up resources is unsustainable. Poor people (and increasingly others as well) are unable to defend themselves against corporate interests and find themselves forced out of the market or into industries which would be considered too dangerous or polluting to be located in rich countries or near the houses and playgrounds of the rich. As resources become scarcer, livelihoods are threatened and competition becomes ever more ruthless. Green politics is therefore a justice issue and an important element in world peace. If we render this world uninhabitable through climate change or the effects of war, everyone will suffer and poor people will suffer first and longest. This is already happening.

Green liberation theology provides a strong basis for a Christian critique of voracious consumerism. At its best, it goes further, questioning the idea that our relationship with non-human nature is simply material and economic. All kinds of people (not just landed gentry and romantic poets) say that they experience something in the midst of nature which touches them deeply. A friend tells me that climbing mountains is her equivalent of going to church. Another says he goes sailing to remake his soul. It is easy to dismiss such experiences or to value them only as commercial opportunities, but there does seem to be something in us which loves the company of non-human nature and pines for it when we are away from it too long. This could be just a physiological response or the effect of cultural conditioning, but many talk still about it in religious terms, as if being in the company of non-human nature can, on occasion, link us to the mystery which is called God.

So there are many good reasons why we should cherish the earth. We are part of nature and, on the whole, it is good for us, both spiritually and materially. More than that, it is essential to our survival. So is this the authentic Christian response which was so badly lacking back in 1972? And if so, why does it stink so horribly of self-interest?

* * *

My third memory is a sequence rather than a single event. I first began to notice non-human nature again – really notice it – while I was researching beliefs about nature in early Christian Ireland.[xv] But while friends waited for me to come up with the goods, ecologically speaking, I found myself in a world so strange and unfamiliar that the first task had to be simply to understand it on its own terms. It was Breandán Ó Madagáin (p.81) in Galway who shooed me away from the library one day with the advice to 'get out in it' down to Clare and see for myself what those early Irish nature poets had been talking about. At around the same time, my health deteriorated and I was advised to take more exercise. I began going for walks. Someone gave me a pair of binoculars and I took them with me every morning, more to give the impression of purposeful activity than for any other reason. What happened took me by surprise. For a start, there were far more birds than I had realised, even within walking distance of the house. Each had its own distinctive voice and manner, and they changed with the seasons: intense cold, and suddenly there were fieldfares. The holes in the riverbank were not rabbit holes after all, but sand martins' nests. I began to see how many other lives had been going on around me for years, in places I thought I knew.

Over the next few years, I got to know relatively undamaged habitats, places where non-human nature lives on, more or less undisturbed. 'This is what the world used to be like,' I thought, though in fact it was only an after-image of wildness, clinging on under heavy protection. When one of the last great wetland areas of western Europe, Coto Doñana in Andalucia, was threatened by a chemical spillage in 1998, I was shocked by the lack of media coverage and scoured the internet for news. While websites listed numbers of species at risk, I was seeing in my mind's eye creatures I knew by name, quietly ingesting mercury and lead. Thousands of hectares of farmland were also contaminated and many farming families and agricultural workers lost their livelihoods. That Sunday, I sat down to write a bidding prayer for the inhabitants of Doñana. It was easy enough to name the people. They were our neighbours, and there was no question but we should pray for them. But what about the herons and the marbled teal? I had begun to question the kind of theology which is concerned only with human interests, but to pray for birds and animals in church still felt strange, like breaking some sort of taboo.

I wondered why I had never heard such a prayer before. Were we supposed to agree with Joseph Rickaby that 'we have no duties of charity, nor duties of any kind, to the lower animals, as neither to sticks nor stones?' because our nature is 'immeasurably above' theirs? C.W. Hume thought not. 'The Christian doctrine,' he replies, 'is that God, whose nature is "immeasurably above" ours, humbled himself for our sake' and 'we are therefore under an obligation to have enough humility and charity, in imitation of his, to concern ourselves actively with the welfare of creatures which we regard as our inferiors. In sealing up the windows of her official mind, the Church has surely erred against their Maker.' We have a 'duty of neighbourliness towards animals,' he says, and this should be reflected regularly in public worship.[xvi]

More recently, Sallie McFague has argued that we must learn to love nature for its own sake, not just for what we can get out of it; we need to stop treating other creatures like objects and begin treating them as other subjects (p.127). This will only happen, she says, if we take time to get to know them, if we learn to look at them not with the 'eye of power', the arrogant controlling gaze which seeks to use the other for its own purposes, but with the loving eye which is truly objective (rather than objecti-*fying*) and able to see other creatures 'in themselves, for themselves' as subjects with their own needs and intentions.[xvii] She admits that this sort of relationship does not come easily. It is not a return to childhood innocence, nor is it the kind of false mysticism which 'finds God in all things' while ignoring the uniqueness of each particular bird or beastie. It is an apprenticeship in knowing and loving the rest of the natural world, for its own sake, not just because it is materially or spiritually useful.

Is this Christian? Is it even possible? It could become deeply *un*christian if we tried to love non-human nature without also recognising the needs of people, and if we loved only beautiful things while ignoring what is ugly or difficult or dull. But that is not the true character of the loving eye. To look lovingly upon other creatures, human and non-human, says McFague, is to begin to see the world as God sees it, taking in the whole complex web of relationships and loving nature exactly as it is. This raises all kinds of difficult questions, and of course there will be tensions. There will be struggles for survival, though it is important to distinguish between the survival of a way of life and the survival of life itself. It is good to be reminded that the bee in the blossom does not belong to us (p.63) but it will be hard to accept any of this if you are living at the sharp end of economic policies which place little or no value on non-human life, or on the lives of poor people or of future generations.

The idea that God cares for the whole community of creatures is there in scripture, though we seem to have forgotten this over the centuries. Look up birds and animals in most Christian reference books and you are likely to find notes on their symbolic meaning, their purpose (to be useful to us), their lack of a soul, their function in pre-Christian worship and ritual; very little about why – or even whether – we should care about them.[xviii] Ralph Hodgson (p.138) famously railed against Christian indifference to animal suffering and Albert Schweitzer (p.45) would mock Western philosophers and theologians for the same failing. Arthur Broome, founder of the Society for the Prevention of Cruelty to Animals (now the RSPCA), was an Anglican clergyman, but this can seem like a drop in the ocean compared to the general climate of exploitation and neglect.[xix] Not that Broome was unique. Care for the non-human nature has a long, quiet history within the church (p.170) but it is a marginal, minority tradition and I have yet to hear it mentioned in any sermon.

Why should this be? The Bible has been read aloud in churches for centuries, and parts of it are much less anthropocentric than we have become. Perhaps we have simply not been listening to those passages which relate to creatures other than ourselves. God's provision in Genesis 1 is for 'everything that has the breath of life' and his promises or covenants (pp.96, 144) often include promises to non-human nature. There are laws designed to protect fields and domestic animals from exhaustion (p.97). The Psalmists celebrate God's 'tender care' towards every creature (p.51, 102) and in Job we find God glorying in his relationship with wild beasts and birds (p.99) far from human habitation. Jesus teaches that God sees even a sparrow fall (p.62) and St Paul includes the whole of nature in his vision of redemption (p.112).

Through making this anthology I have begun hearing the ecological relevance of such passages for the first time. Before that, such environmental awareness as I had came to me mainly by way of everyday life. A childhood experience of wonder gave way to a focus on human nature which only began to broaden out when I started paying better attention to the non-human creatures in my own neighbourhood. Had I grown up in a farming or a fishing community, in daily, gritty, smelly contact with the stuff, my journey would have been different, but perhaps like my mother (who did grow up in such a situation) I would still have retained an instinctive love of nature, however awkward or imperfect.

You may be far ahead of me in this, both in thinking and in lifestyle. The young man from Friends of the Earth certainly was and I would like to apologise to him. Right now, I feel like the young Augustine with his famous prayer 'Give me continence, but not yet'. My twenty-first-century version would be: 'Give me sustainability, but not yet. Let me keep my car, my central heating, my shopping basket full of cheap groceries.' This is not going to be easy. We need to start re-thinking our lives, our belief-systems, as if the rest of nature mattered, re-imagining our place in the scheme of things in the light of the best of our religious traditions and in the light of new theories and discoveries.

We can all do this, but it is also good to watch the professionals, people like Ruth Page who has been trawling these waters for years with apparent fearlessness. Her belief that God is present to all creatures in freedom and love (p.140) has been arrived at without dodging any of the difficult issues and is one of the most interesting and challenging pieces of ecotheology I have read. We can also listen to the experience of Christians in other parts of the world, particularly in non-Western cultures (p.166) where there are different patterns of thinking and relating; and to reports and official teachings, rarely glamorous, but important markers of progress. Finally, we need to listen to what is happening round about us.

* * *

This anthology is meant to move and provoke. It includes some theology in the traditional sense and some extracts from official documents, but it is not meant to be an academic work or a historical account of Christian attitudes to nature, nor is it a collection of ready-made liturgies. These are now available through organisations like Christian Ecology Link (www. christian-ecology.org.uk), the European Christian Environmental Network (www.ecen.org) and the Iona Community has several, in its various books of liturgy, prayer and meditation (www.ionabooks.com). *Cherish the Earth* is intended to be a resource for churches and schools, but it is not just a book for parish leaders and teachers. The environment is perhaps *the* ecumenical issue of our time, and the more I searched, the more I found eloquent material by people of other faiths and those who were reluctant to declare their religious affiliation, even when they obviously had one. Originally, there was going to be a separate section called 'non-Christian perspectives' but that led to all kinds of difficulties, especially with contemporary poets. Who was I to judge the faith-world of someone I barely knew? So I did away with the *cordon sanitaire* between Christian and non-Christian and came to think of this as a kind of gathering, hosted by Christians, but with important contributions from people outside the church.

At times, this makes for jolts and contradictions, and there are different points of view even among the Christians: from the distant-seeming God of R.S. Thomas and Derick Thomson, to the intimate-seeming God of Athanasius and the Chinese Advent hymn. Readers must decide for themselves what is helpful and where tradition needs to be challenged or reaffirmed. I do not mean to imply that differences of theology are unimportant or that one religion is as good as another, but here is an opportunity to listen to each other on a matter which is already making fools of us all. The outlook is international, but since this is a collection made in Scotland, I have given it a suitably local flavour, with poems in Scots and Gaelic as well as from the wider Celtic world. I hope that Welsh and Irish speakers will forgive me for reproducing only the Gaelic in the original. Readers who have trouble with the items in Scots will find a glossary to each in the endnotes. I have always enjoyed hearing different languages and accents, and there is growing evidence for something which governments have always known, namely that people who are able to express themselves publicly in their own language are often in a better position to maintain their own values and perspectives than those who are not. In a world tending towards monoculture, this is surely an advantage, helping to preserve a biodiversity of ideas and imaginative solutions.

It remains only to thank the many writers and copyright-holders who kindly gave me permission to reproduce their work. I am particularly grateful to those who donated poems or gave them at a reduced rate believing that it was all in a good cause. *Cherish* would have been skinny and poor without them. This does not bind anyone to agreement with all I have written here. All kinds of people made suggestions and supported me through the process of collecting. Thank you to all of them, especially to Ruth Burgess, Ruth Page, Michael Regan, Tony Dilworth and everyone at the Scottish Poetry Library. Finally, and as always, my thanks to Bruce who understands what a hillside in Gairloch and an Edinburgh park have in common.

Mary Low
Feast of the Presentation, 21st November 2002

Notes

i   BBC Radio 4, interview with Frank Culbertson, 31 August 2001.

ii   Sallie McFague, *Super, Natural Christians*, SCM, London, 1997, 31–2.

iii   For example, Luke 16:19–31. But even St Paul, at his most world-weary, decides that it is more important to live in this world than flee into the next. Philippians 1:21–3.

iv   Eugene C. Odum, *Fundamentals of Ecology*, Philadelphia, 1953.

v   Published in 1962, this ground-breaking study was one of the first to bring to public awareness the damaging effects of profligate use of chemical pesticides. Dismissed as an alarmist at the time, Carson (1907–64) is now widely respected as a pioneer environmentalist.

vi   *Getting Personal*, SPCK, London, 1995, 3–6. See also Sallie McFague's 'credo' and the beginning of *Life Abundant: rethinking theology and economy for a planet in peril*, Fortress Press, Minneapolis, 2001, 3–24.

vii   *Confessions* X:34.

viii Leonardo Boff, *Cry of the Earth, Cry of the Poor*, Orbis Books, New York, 1997, 180. 'If the Christ has taken shape and consciousness in Jesus, it must be that it already existed in the cosmogenic and anthropogenic process.' Ibid. 177.

ix   First published as *Le Milieu Divin*, Paris, 1957.

x   *Life Abundant*, 10.

xi   Lynn White, 'The historical roots of our ecologic crisis,' *Science*, vol. 155, no. 3767, 10 March 1967, 1204–7; *New Scientist*, vol.48, no.732, 31 December 1970, p.575.

xii   Pope Paul IV, apostolic letter *Octogesima Adveniens*, 1971.

xiii The title of a campaign initiated in 1983 in which the Council called on its members to make public commitments and undertake common action for the sake of 'justice, peace and the integrity of creation'.

xiv McFague, *Life Abundant*, xiv.

xv   See my *Celtic Christianity and Nature: early Irish and Hebridean traditions*, Edinburgh University Press, 1996, reprinted by Polygon, Edinburgh, 1999, ix–xii. Also 'The Natural World in early Christian Ireland: an ecological footnote', in *Celts and Christians,* Mark Atherton and Oliver Davies (eds), University of Wales Press, Cardiff, 2002, 169–203.

xvi *Dictionary of Christian Ethics*, John MacQuarrie (ed), London, 1967, 11–13. A.C. Hume was Director General of the Universities' Foundation for Animal Welfare.

xvii *Super, Natural Christians*, 26–117. The distinction between the loving eye and the arrogant eye comes originally from Marilyn Frye, 'In and out of harm's way: arrogance and love', in *The Politics of Reality: essays in feminist theory*, Trumanberg, New York, 1983, 53–83.

xviii An honourable exception would be John MacQuarrie's *A Dictionary of Christian Ethics*, p.11–3. Thank you to Gerry Hand for drawing my attention to this.

xix The SPCA was the first animal welfare society in the world. Founded by Arthur Broome (1780–1837) its prospectus affirms the 'great moral and Christian obligation of kindness and compassion towards the brute creation'. Its first board included many Christians, laity and clergy, including William Wilberforce. The Archbishop of Canterbury, Donald Coggan, was its president in 1977. Andrew Linzey and Tom Regan, *Compassion for Animals*, SPCK, London, 1998, iv, xxiii.

APPROACHES

Night herons

It was after a day's rain:
the street facing the west
was lit with growing yellow;
the black road gleamed.

First one child looked and saw
and told another.
Face after face, the windows
flowered with eyes.

It was like a long fuse lighted,
the news travelling.
No one called out loudly;
everyone said 'Hush.'

The light deepened; the wet road
answered in daffodil colours,
and down its centre
walked two tall herons.

Stranger than wild birds, even,
what happened to those faces;
suddenly believing in something,
they smiled and opened.

Children thought of fountains,
circuses, swans feeding:
women remembered words
spoken when they were young.

Everyone said 'Hush;'
no one spoke loudly;
but suddenly the herons
rose and were gone. The light faded.

—Judith Wright

Bright moon, scattered stars, so solitary is creation. The universe which God has created is especially silent on this night. It waits with bated breath for the Lord of Creation to return.

The universe belongs to him. It is his home.

Silence reigns supreme. The flowers of the field sway gently in the moon-light. This night, the vast earth awaits the homecoming of our Creator God.

The vast earth and open fields belong to God. They are his home.

Bethlehem lies dreaming. In his gentle mother's arms, the babe sleeps peacefully this night. The City of David awaits the homecoming of David's descendant.

The town of Bethlehem belongs to him. It is his home.

My bones, my flesh, my blood, my lungs and my heart, were all made by his hand: this night, my heart is at peace, awaiting my Creator's return.

My heart belongs to him. It is his home.

> —Advent Prayer. Anon., China

The bonnie broukit bairn

Mars is braw in crammasy,
Venus in a green silk goun,
The auld mune shak's her gowden feathers,
Their starry talk's a wheen o'blethers,
Nane for thee a thochtie sparin',
Earth, thou bonnie broukit bairn!

> *But greet, an in your tears ye'll droun*
> *The haill clanjamfrie!*

> —Hugh MacDiarmid

Today

Today came spring
                                    -ing
took me by surprise,
leapt and
bowled me over
like a big
daft dog.

On the train rolling through
snowcovered fields, the
bright sun scudding beside me
                                    along
touching me awake to see.

Today it came
with crocuses open by
hardfrozen tractortracks
with daffodils, bent by the snow
but Trumpeting

with O the Sun
and even, God, lambs
Today came Spring

—Alan Spence

Oh Lord our God, if you are so lovely in your creatures, how exceedingly beautiful and ravishing you must be in yourself.

—Henry Suso

Sweeney's island hermitage

Carraig Alistair
home of seagulls
miserable, O Creator
cold for its guests

Carraig Alistair
bell-shaped rock
too sheer by half
nose to the waves

Wet these beds
where I have my dwelling
Little did I think it
a rock of refuge

—*Anon., middle-Irish*

Ealghol: dà shealladh

Choimhead mi an t-seann chairt-phuist,
na taighean mar fhàs às an talamh,
na h-aonaichean nam baidealan os an cionn,
nan comharra air mòrachd Dhè,
mus d'rinneadh goireas de bheanntan,
no sgaradh eadar obair is fois,
eadar an naomh is an saoghalta …
is shìn mi chun a' bhodaich i.

'Eil sin cur cianalas ort, a Lachaidh?'
dh'fhaighnich mi, 's e na thosd ga sgrùdadh.
'Hoigh, òinseach, chan eil idir!
'S e cuimhne gun aithne a bh'agam oirrese,'
is stiùir e ri bò ar thùs an deilbh.
'Siud a'Leadaidh Bhuidhe, an dàrna laogh aig a'Leadaidh Ruadh –
dh'aithnichinn, fhios agad, bò sam bith
a bhuineadh dhan àite seo rim bheò-sa.'

Elgol: two views

I looked at the old post-card,
the houses like a growth from the soil,
the peaks towering above them,
a sign of the majesty of God,
before an amenity was made of mountains,
or a divide between work and play,
between the sacred and the secular …
and I passed the picture to the old man.

'Does it make you sad, Lachie?' I asked
as he scrutinised it in silence.
'Sad? Bah! Not at all!
I couldn't place her for a moment,'
and he pointed to the cow in the foreground.
'That's the Yellow Lady, the Red Lady's second calf –
I'd know any cow, you see,
that belonged here in my life-time.'

—*Meg Bateman*

Paw marks

Just as a housewife who has scrubbed out the parlour, takes care that the door is left shut so that the dog may not get in and spoil the work she has done by the marks of his paws, so do European thinkers watch carefully that no animals run about in the fields of their ethics. The stupidities that they are guilty of in trying to raise it to a principle border on the incredible. Either they leave out altogether all sympathy for animals, or they take care that it shrinks to a mere afterthought which means nothing. If they admit anything more than that, they think themselves obliged to produce elaborate justifications, or even excuses, for so doing. It seems as if Descartes with his dictum that animals are mere machines had bewitched the whole of European philosophy.

—*Albert Schweitzer*

THANKS AND PRAISE

Be exalted, O God, above the heavens;
let your glory be over all the earth.

—*Psalm 57:11*

Laud ye the Lord

Halleluia! Laud the Lord himsel frae the lift;
laud him frae the heighest heights:
Laud him, a' errand-rinners o' his ain,
laud him, a' hosts o' his.
Laud him, baith sun and mune;
laud him, a' starns o' light:
Laud him, ye lift o' lifts;
an ye fludes owre the hevins' height ...
Laud ye the Lord, frae yirth,
gryfes an' ilk awesome howe:

Lowe an' hail; snaw an' mist;
whirlin' blast that wirks his bidden:
Heigh heights, and a' ye knowes;
frutefu' stoks and ilka cedar:
Brute o' the field, an' beiss o' the fauld;
wurblin worm, an' fliean feddyr:
Kings o' the yirth, an' a' peopil;
provosts, an' a' right-rechters o' the lan':
Baith lads an' lasses: auld folk an' bairns …
Laud till the Lord gie ye!

—*Psalm 148*

Canticle of Creation

Most high, almighty, good Lord,
to you belong praise and glory and honour
and every blessing.

To you alone do they belong, O Most High
for no one is worthy to pronounce your name.

Praise to you, Lord, through all your creatures,
and especially through our noble Brother Sun,
through whom we have daylight and illumination
for he is beautiful and radiant and dazzling
and he reveals to us something of yourself.

Praise to you, Lord, through Sister Moon and the stars
which you have set in the heavens,
bright and precious and beautiful.

Praise to you, Lord, through Brother Wind
and air and clouds and stillness and every kind of weather
by which you uphold creation.

Praise to you, Lord, through Sister Water
who is very useful and humble and precious and pure.

Praise to you, Lord, through Brother Fire
through whom you light up the darkness
for he is beautiful and cheery and vigorous and mighty.

Praise to you, Lord, for Sister Earth, our mother
who feeds us and governs us
and produces all kinds of fruits and colourful flowers and herbs.

Praise to you, Lord, for all who forgive each other through your love,
and who endure illness and tribulation.

Blessed are they who endure it peaceably
for you will honour them, O Most High.

Praise to you, Lord, for our sister Death
for no living body can escape from her.
Wretched are they who die in mortal sin.
Blessed are they who are found doing your will
for the second death will not harm them.

Praise and bless my Lord and give thanks to him
and serve him with great humility.

—St Francis of Assisi

Mohawk prayer

Thank you, Creator of the universe, for the people gathered around us today. We give thanks for the things of the earth that give us the means of life.

Thank you for the plants, animals and birds that we use as food and medicine.

Thank you for the natural world, in which we find the means to be clothed and housed.

Thank you Lord, for the ability to use these gifts of the natural world.

Help us to see our place among these gifts, not to squander them or think of them as a means of selfish gain.

May we respect the life of all you have made. May our spirits be strengthened by using only what we need, and may we use our strength to help those who need us. Amen.

—*Sue Ellen Herne*

Glorious Lord

Hail to you, glorious Lord!
May church and chancel praise you,
May chancel and church praise you,
May plain and hillside praise you,
May the three springs praise you,
Two higher than the wind and one above the earth,
May darkness and light praise you,
May the cedar and the sweet fruit-tree praise you.
Abraham praised you, the founder of faith,
May life everlasting praise you,

May the birds and beasts praise you
May the stubble and the grass praise you.
Aaron and Moses praised you,
May male and female praise you,
May the seven days and the stars praise you,
May the lower and upper air praise you,
May books and letters praise you,
May the sand and the earth praise you,
May all good things created praise you,
And I too shall praise you, Lord of glory,
Hail to you, glorious Lord.

—Anon. Welsh

Even the sparrow

How lovely is your dwelling-place,
O Lord of hosts.
My soul longs, indeed faints,
for the courts of the Lord;
my heart and my flesh sing for joy
to the living God.

Even the sparrow finds a home
and the swallow a nest for herself
where she may lay her young
at your altars, O Lord of hosts.
Happy are those who live in your house,
ever singing your praise.

—Psalm 84:1–4

Eòsai bu chòir a mholadh

Bu cho fus a dh'Iosa
an crann crìon ùradh
's an crann ùr a' crìonadh,
nam b'e rùn a dhèanadh.
Eòsai! Eòsai! Eòsai!
Eòsai! bu chòir a mholadh.

Ni bheil lus an làr
nach bheil làn d'a thoradh,
ni bheil cruth an tràigh
nach bheil làn d'a shonas.
Eòsai! Eòsai! Eòsai!
Eòsai! bu chòir a mholadh.

Ni bheil creubh am fairge,
ni bheil dearg an abhainn,
ni bheil càil an fhailbhe,
nach bheil dearbh d'a mhaitheas.
Eòsai! Eòsai! Eòsai!
Eòsai! bu chòir a mholadh.

Ni bheil ian air sgèith
ni bheil reul an adhar,
ni bheil sian fo'n ghrèin.
nach tog sgeul d'a mhaitheas.
Eòsai! Eòsai! Eòsai!
Eòsai! bu chòir a mholadh.

Jesus, worthy of praise

It would be as easy for Jesus
to renew the withered tree
as to wither the green one
if he so wished.
Jesus, Jesus, Jesus
Jesus, worthy of praise

There is not a plant in the ground
but is full of his fruitfulness
There is not a living thing on the beach
but is full of his blessing
Jesus, Jesus, Jesus
Jesus, worthy of praise

There is not a creature in the sea
there is not a fish in the river
there is nothing in the heavens
but is proof of his goodness
Jesus, Jesus, Jesus
Jesus, worthy of praise

There is not a bird on the wing
there is not a star in the sky
there is not an element under the sun
but tells of his goodness
Jesus, Jesus, Jesus
Jesus, worthy of praise

　　　—Anon.

Exactly as He wishes it to be

The Qur'an tells us that everything that Allah has created in the universe completely submits to his will. So a rock is perfectly the rock that Allah commands it to be, the tree is exactly what Allah commands it to be, and wild animals such as the deer, the camel or the tiger are all exactly as Allah wishes them to be. Everything in creation is obedient to Allah in this way, no matter whether it is non-living like the air, the earth or the oceans, or living like the animals, the plants, the bacteria and the fungi. It makes no difference whether something is microscopic or immense. The particles of atoms and the massive galaxies of outer space are all obedient. And because each thing that Allah created is exactly as He wishes it to be, then everything in creation works properly and the whole creation fits together in a meaningful way. Creation is therefore sacred. The Prophet Mohammed, peace be upon Him, said: 'The whole of this earth is a mosque,' that is, a place of worship.

—*Yunus Negus*

Through heaven and earth and sea, through wood and stone, through relics and Church buildings and the Cross, through angels and people, through all creation visible and invisible, I offer veneration and honour to the Creator and Master and Maker of all things and to him alone.

—*Leontius of Cyprus*

KYRIE

Barley field

Rows of perfect plants
dark green
stretch out
to meet the pristine blue
of summer sky,
a nursery picture
almost beautiful
in its uniformity.

No sound is heard
no hum of bees
no call, no song of birds
no added colour from the butterfly
but round the field
a damaged food chain
reaches to the arctic.

—*Dorcas Symms*

Faith in a seed

The industrialised world depends entirely on crops and cultivation practices imported from what we now call the Third World (though evidently it was actually First) … Those who know the seed business are well aware that our shallow gene bank is highly vulnerable; when a crop strain succumbs all at once to a new disease … researchers must return to the more diverse original strains for help. So we still rely on the gigantic insurance policy provided by the genetic variability in the land races, which continue to be hand-sown and harvested, year in and year out, by farmers in those mostly poor places from which our crops arose.

Unbelievably, we are now engaged in a serious effort to cancel that insurance policy.

It happens like this. Let's say you are an Ethiopian farmer growing a land race of wheat – a wildly variable, husky mongrel crop that has been in your family for hundreds of years. You always lose some to wind and weather, but the rest still comes through every year. Lately, though, you've been hearing about a kind of Magic Wheat that grows six times bigger than your crop, is easier to harvest and contains vitamins that aren't found in ordinary wheat. And amazingly enough, by special arrangement with the government, it's free.

Readers who have even the slightest acquaintance with fairy tales will already know there is trouble ahead in this story. The Magic Wheat grows well the first year, but its rapid, overly green growth attracts a startling number of pests. You see insects on this crop that never ate wheat before, in the whole of your family's history. You watch, you worry. You realise that you're going to have to spray a pesticide to get this crop through to harvest. You're not so surprised to learn that by special arrangement with the government, the same company that gave you the seed for free can sell you the pesticide you need. It's a good pesticide, they use it all the time in America, but it costs money you don't have, so you'll have to borrow against next year's crop.

The second year, you will be visited by a terrible drought, and your crop will not survive to harvest at all; every stalk dies. Magic wheat from America doesn't know beans about Ethiopian drought. The end.

Actually, if the drought arrived in year two and the end came that quickly, in this real-life fairy tale you'd be very lucky, because chances are good you'd still have some of your family-line seed around. It would be much more disastrous if the drought waited until the eighth or ninth year to wipe you out, for then you'd have no wheat left at all, Magic or otherwise. Seed banks, even if they're eleven thousand years old, can't survive for more than a few years on the shelf. If they aren't grown out as crops year after year, they die – or else get ground into flour and baked and eaten – and then this product of a thousand hands and careful selection is just gone, once and for all ...

While agricultural companies have purchased, stored, and patented certain genetic materials from old crops, they cannot engineer a crop, ever, that will have the resilience of land races under a wide variety of conditions of moisture, predation, and temperature. Genetic engineering is the antithesis of variability because it removes the wild card – that beautiful thing called sex – from the equation.

... I was trained as a biologist, and I can appreciate the challenge and the technical mastery involved in isolating, understanding, and manipulating genes. I can think of fascinating things I'd like to do as a genetic engineer. But I only have to stand still for a minute and watch the outcome of thirty million years' worth of hummingbird evolution transubstantiated before my eyes into nest and egg to get knocked down to size. I have held in my hand the germ of a plant engineered to grow, yield its crop, and then murder its own embryos, and there I glimpsed the malevolence that can lie in the heart of a profiteering enterprise. There once was a time when Thoreau wrote, 'I have great faith in a seed. Convince me that you have a seed there, and I am prepared to expect wonders.'

By the power vested in everything living, let us keep to that faith. I'm a scientist who thinks it wise to enter the doors of creation not with a lion-tamer's whip and chair, but with the reverence humankind has tradition-ally summoned for entering places of worship: a temple, a mosque, or a cathedral. A sacred grove, as ancient as time.

—*Barbara Kingsolver*

The changes

A peewit came
this spring to the island
in snowflakes, daffodils and the wind.

Usually a whole gale of them blow in,
their voices like children's, their flight
soft and dipping across the sea fields.

But this year
only one came back
in the wild sunlight of March.

We watched and waited
we listened in the mornings
but there was just one peewit

Strange and hopeless
upon the clay dark of the moorland
calling and calling without end.

—*Kenneth C. Steven*

Hear the word of the Lord, O people of Israel;
for the Lord has an indictment
against the inhabitants of the land.
There is no faithfulness or loyalty,
and no knowledge of God in the land.
Swearing, lying and murder,
and stealing and adultery break out;
bloodshed follows bloodshed.
Therefore the land mourns,
and all who live in it languish;
together with the wild animals
and the birds of the air,
even the fish of the sea are perishing.

—*Hosea 4:1–3*

No longer in ignorance

Our ancestors sinned in ignorance; they were taught ... that the world, with all it contains, was made for humans, and that the lower orders of creation have no claims whatever upon us. But we no longer have the excuse of saying that we do not know; we do know that organic life on this planet is all woven of one stuff, and if we are children of our Heavenly Father, it must be true, as Christ told us, that no sparrow falls to the ground without his care. The new knowledge has revolutionised our ideas of our relations to other living creatures who share the world with us, and it is our duty to consider seriously what this knowledge should mean for us in matters of conduct.

—*William Ralph Inge*

The voice of God – heard by one who was prayerful

The fish in the torrent	Does not belong to you
The bird in the air	Does not belong to you
The bee in the blossom	Does not belong to you
The dew in the dawn	Does not belong to you
The dark of night	Does not belong to you
The red of feather	Does not belong to you
The soaking rain	Does not belong to you
The lapping wave	Does not belong to you
The tight-lipped horse	Does not belong to you
The lofty height	Does not belong to you
The level plain	Does not belong to you
Nothing on the Earth	
Or in the Sky	Belongs to you

—Brent Hodgson

A disaster

There came news of a word.
Crow saw it killing men. He ate well.
He saw it bulldozing
Whole cities to rubble. Again he ate well.
He saw its excreta poisoning seas.
He became watchful.
He saw its breath burning whole lands
To dusty char.
He flew clear and peered.

The word oozed its way, all mouth,
Earless, eyeless.
He saw it sucking the cities
Like the nipples of a sow
Drinking out all the people
Till there were none left,
All digested inside the word.

Ravenous, the word tried its great lips
On the earth's bulge, like a giant lamprey –
There it started to suck,

But its effort weakened.
It could digest nothing but people.
So there it shrank, wrinkling weaker,
Puddling
Like a collapsing mushroom.
Finally, a drying salty lake.
Its era was over,
All that remained of it a brittle desert
Dazzling with the bones of earth's people
Where crow walked and mused.

—*Ted Hughes*

Urnaigh Iain Ruaidh

Tha Thu ann a shin
'na do shuidhe air a rìgh-chathair
's chan eil nì dol seachad ort;
cuige rèist a leig Thu dhuinne
a dhol cho fada air seacharan,
carson a rinn Thu foighidinn
nuair a dh'èisd sinn ri buille na cuisle,
nuair a thuirt an t-sannt ruinn
"Gabh 's na diùlt,"
nuair a rag an uaill ar cogais?
Cuine dh'fhàg Thu 'n dall-bhrat air d'eaglais
Aig àird a' mheadhon-latha,
's a mhùch Thu choinneal
nuair a bha sinn a'sireadh d'altair?
Sinne th'air moglachadh 'na do lìon,
Na caomhn do sgian oirnn.

Red John's prayer

There You are
sitting on the throne,
noticing everything;
why then have You let us
go so far astray,
why were you patient
when we listened to the pulse's beat,
when greed said to us
'Take, do not refuse,'

when pride hardened our conscience?
Why have You let your church stay blindfold
in the bright sun of midday,
and smothered the candle
when we were seeking Your altar?
We who are entangled in Your net,
do not spare the knife on us.

—*Ruaraidh MacThòmais / Derick Thomson*

Confession

We confess our sins, and the sins of our society,
in the misuse of God's creation.

God our Father, we are sorry
for the times when we have used your gifts carelessly,
and acted ungratefully.
Hear our prayer, and in your mercy:

Forgive us and help us

We enjoy the fruits of the harvest,
but sometimes forget that you have given them to us.
Father, in your mercy:

Forgive us and help us

We belong to a people who are full and satisfied,
but ignore the cry of the hungry.
Father, in your mercy:

Forgive us and help us

We are thoughtless,
and do not care enough for the world you have made.
Father, in your mercy:

Forgive us and help us

We store up goods for ourselves alone,
as if there were no God and no heaven.
Father in your mercy:

Forgive us and help us

> —*Church of England Prayer Book*

Cry of the Earth, cry of the poor

For four centuries all societies of the world have been held hostage to a myth, the myth of progress and of uninterrupted growth. Countries must show higher rates in the production of goods and services every year. That is the standard for judging whether a country is developed, under-developed or just plain backward. Such progress follows the iron logic of maximising benefits while minimising costs and the use of time ... All productive forces have been harnessed to draw from the Earth all that it can provide. A systematic assault has been mounted on its wealth in the soil, the subsoil, the air, the sea and the outer atmosphere. War has been waged on all fronts. Victims have been produced on an unprecedented scale: the working class oppressed world-wide, peripheral nations exploited, the overall quality of life in decline and nature plundered.

> —*Leonardo Boff*

To a mouse

On turning up her nest with the plough
November 1785

Wee sleekit, cowrin, tim'rous beastie
O, what a panic's in thy breastie!
Thou need na start awa' sae hasty
    wi' bickering brattle!
I wad be laith to rin an' chase thee
    wi' murderin' pattle!

I'm truly sorry man's dominion
has broken nature's social union,
an' justifies that ill opinion
    which makes thee startle
at me, thy poor, earth-born companion
    an' fellow mortal!

I doubt na, whyles, but thou may thieve;
What then? Poor beastie, thou maun live!
A daimen icker in a thrave
    's a sma' request;
I'll get a blessin wi' the lave,
    an never miss't!

Thy wee-bit housie, too, in ruin!
Its silly wa's the win's are strewin!
An' naething, now, to big a new ane,
    o' foggage green!
An' bleak December's win's ensuin,
    baith snell an' keen!

Thou saw the fields laid bare an' waste,
an' weary winter comin' fast,
an' cozie here, beneath the blast,
    thou thought to dwell,
till crash! The cruel coulter past
    out thro' thy cell.

That wee bit heap o' leaves and stibble,
has cost thee monie a weary nibble!
Now thou's turned out, for a' thy trouble,
    but house or hald,
to thole the winter's sleety dribble
    an' canreuch cauld!

But Mousie, thou art no thy lane,
in proving foresight may be vain;
the best-laid schemes o' mice an' men
    gang aft agley,
an' lea'e us nought but grief an' pain,
    for promised joy!

Still thou art blest, compared wi' me!
The present only toucheth thee:
But och! I backward cast my e'e,
    on prospects drear!
An' forward, tho' I canna see
    I guess an' fear!

    —*Robert Burns*

Sorry

Dear loving Father,
we are sorry …
for destroying your world.

We are sorry …
for the pollution of the sea
and for pouring gallons of oil into it every year.

We are sorry …
for the car fumes in the atmosphere,
for acid rain and all the things it destroys.

We are sorry …
for the destruction of animals and their homes,
and for litter in the streets.

Please help us to make our world a better place.
Amen.

—Geraldine Murphy, aged 10

The world as it was

Most people would regard the life of Travellers as anything but enviable. I, however, would love to be able to go back again. Back to the world as it was then. When one could drink the cool, clean, pure water of mountain burns. Eat the fruits of any byway hedges, the young leaves of hawthorn, and later the fruit. Arnuts, sooracks (a green leaf which is most pleasantly sour), blaeberries, cranberries, brambles and wild gooseberries. The heads of corn, wheat, and barley too, could be rubbed between the hands, then blown on gently to get rid of the husks and eaten. Rabbits were delicious, as were brown trout. All were free from disease and poisons.

The world was as yet unpolluted. Our part of it was, anyway. We could pitch our tents in places of unrivalled beauty, right in the heart of the countryside, enjoying our bairns and our friends. The nests of harvest mice, wrens, robins and woodpeckers we could show our weans. Those little homes would defy any human builder to equal. We could shift to clean ground after a thunderstorm.

Now I can hear a lot of you say 'Yes, and muck it up with your dirt.' I admit lots of Travellers did exactly that, but within a year Mother Earth had sucked the dirt into her large re-processing belly and turned it into a nourishing diet for herself.

Yes, I am much more than grateful that I knew the world as it was then. Now it is impossible to get anything to eat which is pure and not full of all manner of chemical poisons. Nor can one drink from any burn the ice-cold sparkling water …

—*Betsy White*

On the train

It is so frosty a morning
with nothing to protect the earth
from the coldness of space.

Whiteness mutes the colours
and softens the edges of dark trees.

Mists blow across the flat lands,
and heat where it rises magnifies in the air
catching the colour of the rising sun.
I enjoy a great joy
travelling effortlessly
watching the world
through the train window.

And on the paper in front of me
waiting to be read
the story of Kimberley and Belinda
the twins who have been sold – twice.

—*Sandra Goodwill*

Obijway prayer

Grandfather,
look at our brokenness.
We know that in all creation
only the human family
has strayed from the sacred way.
We know that we are the ones
who are divided.
And we are the ones
who must come back together
to walk in the sacred way.
Grandfather, Sacred One,
teach us to love compassion and honour
that we may heal the earth
and heal each other.

—*Art Solomon*

A child's pet

When I sailed out of Baltimore,
    with twice a thousand head of sheep,
they would not eat, they would not drink,
    but bleated o'er the deep.

Inside the pens we crawled each day,
    to sort the living from the dead;
and when we reached the Mersey's mouth,
    had lost five hundred head.

Yet every night and day one sheep,
    that had no fear of man nor sea,
stuck through the bars its pleading face
    and it was stroked by me.

And to the sheep-men standing near,
    'You see,' I said, 'this one tame sheep?
It seems a child has lost her pet,
    and cried herself to sleep.'

So every time we passed it by,
    sailing to England's slaughter-house,
eight ragged sheep-men – tramps and thieves –
    would stroke that sheep's black nose.

—*W.H. Davies*

Let us not be in despair over human sin

Merciful God, let us not be in despair over human sin.
Help us to love one another even in our sins
for that is already the semblance of your love.
Help us to love all of your creation,
the whole of it: every grain of sand,
every leaf, every ray of your light.
May we love the animals, the plants, everything.
Help us to perceive your mystery in things
and to understand it more and more each day.

Help us to love the animals.
You have given them the rudiments of thought
and untroubled joy. Let us not trouble them,
torture them, or deprive them of their joy.
Let us not go against your intent.
Let us not exalt ourselves above the animals:
for they are without sin, while we, in our majesty
defile the earth by our appearance on it
and leave traces of our defilement behind us.
Help us to love children especially,
for they are a sort of guidance to us.
Woe to the man or woman who offends a child.

Help us to see that everything, like the ocean,
flows and comes into contact with everything else.
We touch it in one place and it reverberates
at the other end of the world.

Let us be consumed by your universal love
as though in a sort of ecstasy.
Help us to set great store by this ecstasy
however absurd people may think it.
Let us be glad as children.
Let human sin not trouble us in our work.

—After Dostoyevsky

Our brothers, the animals

O God, enlarge within us the sense of fellowship with all living things, our brothers, the animals, to whom you gave the earth as their home in common with us.

We remember with shame that in the past we have exercised the high dominion of man with ruthless cruelty, so that the voice of the earth, which should have gone up to you in song, has been a groan of travail.

May we realise that they live not for us alone, but for themselves and for you, and that they love the sweetness of life.

—Attributed to St Basil the Great

The hornie-golach

When the Lord created Heaven and Earth
He did the wark richt brawly.
Sae hoo in a' the wide, wide warld
Did he mak the creepie-crawlie?

My hert gaes oot tae the hawk in the lift,
Tae the fishes in the sea,
But the love o' the hornie-golach
Is no' for the likes o' me.

There are some o' God's craturs I can lo'e
And ithers that I may thole
It grieves me that o' Creation's wark
I canna lo'e the whole.

I maun try my Makar's patience,
For I'm awfu' slow tae learn
Tae lo'e a' men like my brithers
An' no wish the wicked herm.

'Tae ken a's tae forgi'e a','
I've heard, and maun tak heed,
But it's hard tae cry doon God's benison
For purveyors o' spite and greed.

Sae come you here, Wee Hornie
Na, dinna skitter awa',
And I'll admire your six braw legs,
If ye'll forgi'e my twa.

—*Eunice M. Buchanan*

God of everlasting love,
who is eternally forgiving
pardon and restore us,
and make us one with you
in your new creation.
Amen

—*RSPCA Order of Service*

GLORIA

Creativity

'Let me show you something beautiful'
– ritually opening her palm:
a little feather, mostly black,
though touched with grey and brown,
and on its edge the magic yellow
that made me catch my breath.

The yellow brush-stroke made no sense,
nor balance, shape nor form:
Only the artist could foresee
the pattern 'twould build
joining its fellows on the outspread wing
to make an oriental fan,
the glory of the living bird:
Goldfinch – God's finch.

—*Breandán Ó Madagáin*

From a roof in Brooklyn

From the age of fifteen until the age of twenty-one he lived in the apartment world of his aunt's whispery talking and his uncle's coughs and brooding silence, and he did not know which was more frightening. For a while after his cousin's death he thought his family had somehow been singled out for a special curse. But he talked to friends and found that throughout the neighbourhood ran a twisting river of random events: parents died in slow or sudden ways, children were killed, relatives slipped young from life. The world seemed a strangely terrifying place when you really thought about it. He tried not to think about it too often.

Sometimes to get away from thinking about it he fled to the roof of the apartment house. There, on the cracked and reeking tar paper, he would sit with his back to the brick wall of the stairwell and gaze up across the adjoining rooftops to the sky. Usually it was a smoky stench-filled sky, but on occasion it was clear. One night he saw the vast heaven of stars clear as he had never seen it before, stretching from one end of the city to the other. It was a cool summer night, and as he sat there he heard a soft whining sound and a stirring in the darkness. He was about sixteen at the time, a boy of the streets, not easily given to fear. In the corner of the roof, near a cluster of pipes, vents, and bubble-like protrusions, he found a bitch whelping her pups. She was a black mongrel with a white spot over one eye, and she growled softly as he approached her. He watched the pups come, listened to her soft whimpers, saw her tear and lick off the sacks, clean the pups, push them aside, lie back, and wait for the next. He had never seen life being born before. He knew the street talk about pricks and cunts, had read the porno books passed around in the school yards, seen the photographs of the various positions. But the birth of these pups stirred him in a strange way. He saw them emerge from the organ that he and his friends would talk about with leers on the street. But here on the roof the bitch and her body seemed filled with a singular radiance. Life was being created before his eyes. He trembled, soared, wanted to shout and weep, and remained very still. He reached out to touch one of the newborn pups, and the bitch raised her head and bared her teeth. Overhead the star-filled sky seemed to drop down upon him. He felt caught up in the life of heaven and earth, in the mystery of creation, in the pain and inexhaustible glory of this single moment. He wanted to hold the bitch to himself, caress her, caress something. Instead he reached up and brushed his hand across the sky and felt, actually felt, the achingly exquisitely cool dry velvet touch of starry heaven upon his fingers. He cried a little and shivered in the chill air. Finally, he thought it time to go back down, his aunt would become concerned about him.

—*Chaim Potok*

The ancient wood

The old wood, look, is growing again,
 On every side life is flooding back
Though it's been felled, cut down to feed inferno
 In the trenches of France for four black years.

Four hideous years of mud and bloodshed
 Four deadly years 'mid steel and bomb,
Old years, old years to break Marged's heart
 Years to wither the soul of Twm.

But look, the ancient wood's growing again,
 The scab is lifting cleanly from the cut ...
Though governors of men and their inventors
 Contrive more weapons of damnation yet.

O that gentle wood, I could weep tears,
    So silly sooth your faith in human good,
Despite every grief, so eagerly awaiting
    The hour that reveals us Sons of God.

    —Waldo Williams

God's grandeur

The world is charged with the grandeur of God.
It will flame out, like shining from shook foil;
it gathers to a greatness, like the ooze of oil
crushed. Why do men then now not reck his rod?
Generations have trod, have trod, have trod;
and all is seared with trade; bleared, smeared with toil;
and wears man's smudge and shares man's smell: the soil
is bare now, nor can foot feel, being shod.

And for all this, nature is never spent;
there lives the dearest freshness deep down things;
and though the last lights off the black West went
oh, morning, at the brown brink eastward, springs –
because the Holy Ghost over the bent
world broods with warm breast and with ah! bright wings.

    —Gerard Manley Hopkins

The light trap

Homesick for the other animals
at midnight, in the soft midsummer dark,
we rigged a sail of light amidst
the apple trees beyond your mother's lawn
and counted moths.

This was our first experiment
in guesswork, with a car-torch and a stolen
bedsheet from the upstairs linen press:
our faces smudged with shadow in the lucent
undergrowth, the powder on our wrists

subtle and sweet as graphite, as we named
the shapes we recognised: Merveille-du-jour;
Sycamore; Mother Shipton: Silver Y;
Crimson-and-gold; Old Lady; Angle Shades.

—John Burnside

Rainbow

When you see
de rainbow
you know
God know
wha he doing –
one big smile
across the sky –
I tell you
God got style
the man got style

When you see
raincloud pass
and de rainbow
make a show
I tell you
is God doing
limbo
the man doing
limbo

But sometimes
you know
when I see
de rainbow
so full of glow
& curving
like she bearing child

I does want to know
if God
ain't a woman

If that is so
the woman got style
man she got style

—*John Agard*

Masai fire blessing

Thank you, Father, for your free gift of fire
because it is through fire that you draw near to us.
It is with fire that you constantly bless us.
Our Father, bless this fire today.
With your power, enter into it.
Make this fire a worthy thing,
a thing that carries your blessing.
Let it become a reminder of your love.

Make the life of these people to be baptised like this fire.
A thing that shines for the sake of the people.
A thing that shines for your sake.
Father, heed this sweet-smelling smoke.
Make their life also sweet-smelling,
a thing sweet-smelling that rises to God,
a holy thing,
a thing fitting for you.

—*Anon.*

O God
Whenever I listen to the voice of anything you have made –
the rustling of the trees
the trickling of water
the cries of birds
the flickering of shadow
the roar of the wind
the song of the thunder
I hear it saying:
God is One!
Nothing can be compared with God.

—*Attributed to Rabi'a al-Adawiyya*

Miracle enough

I like to walk alone on country paths, rice plants and wild grasses on both sides, putting each foot down on the earth in mindfulness, knowing that I walk on the wondrous earth. In such moments, existence is a miraculous and mysterious reality. People usually consider walking on water or in thin air a miracle. But I think the real miracle is not to walk either on water or in thin air, but to walk on the earth.

—*Thich Nat Hanh*

West African harvest thanksgiving

Lord of lords, Creator of all things,
God of all things, God over all gods,
God of sun and rain, you created the earth with a thought
and us with your breath.
Lord, we brought in the harvest.
The rain watered the earth,
the sun drew cassava and corn out of the clay.
Your mercy showered blessing after blessing over our lands.
Creeks grew into rivers; swamps became lakes.
Healthy fat cows graze on the green sea of the savanna.
The rain smoothed out the clay walls:
the mosquitoes perished in the high waters.
Lord, the yam is fat like meat, the cassava melts on the tongue, oranges
burst their peels, dazzling and bright.
Lord, nature gives thanks, your creatures give thanks.
Your praise rises in us like a great river.
Lord of lords, Creator, Provider,
we thank you in the name of Jesus Christ.

—*Anon.*

O taste and see

Leader: God, you have given us all kinds of plants
those that bear grain and those that bear fruit.

All: *O taste and see that the Lord is good*

You have given us your Word and Law sweeter than honey
sweeter than honey dripping from the comb.

O taste and see that the Lord is good

You have given us manna in the wilderness of our wandering
and our daily bread to sustain us.

O taste and see that the Lord is good

You have given us:
the heavenly smell of roasted coffee
and the green, rooted scent of gardens dripping rain;
the rush of sugar and the smack of saltiness
the touch and feel of summer breezes
and the warm embrace of close friends;
the sound of song thrushes and herring gulls
pianos and choirs, tubas and skirling bagpipes
playing drunken reels at parties

O taste and see that the Lord is good

—Neil Paynter

Augustine on the beauty of Creation

How could any description do justice to all these blessings?
The manifold diversity of beauty in sky and earth and sea;
the abundance of light, and its miraculous loveliness
in sun and moon and stars;
the dark shades of woods, the colour and fragrance of flowers
the multitudinous varieties of birds
with their songs and their bright plumage;
the countless different species of living creatures
of all shapes and sizes, amongst whom it is the smallest in bulk
that moves our greatest wonder –
for we are more astonished at the activities of the tiny ants and bees
than at the immense bulk of whales.
Then there is the mighty spectacle of the sea itself,
putting on its changing colours like different garments,
now green, with all the many varied shades, now purple, now blue.
Moreover what a delightful sight it is when stormy
giving added pleasure to the spectator because of the agreeable thought
that he is not a sailor tossed and heaved about on it!
Think too of the abundant supply of food
everywhere to satisfy our hunger,
the variety of flavours to suit our pampered taste,
lavishly distributed by the riches of nature
not produced by the skill and labour of cooks!
Think, too, of all the resources for the preservation of health
or for its restoration,
the welcome alternation of day and night,

the soothing coolness of the breezes,
all the material for clothing provided by plants and animals.
Who could give a complete list of these natural blessings? ...
And these are all the consolations of mankind under condemnation
not the rewards of the blessed. What then will those rewards be,
if the consolations are so many and so wonderful?

—*St Augustine*

READINGS & COMMENTARIES

Everything that has the breath of life

So God created humankind in his image, in the image of God he created them; male and female he created them. God blessed them, and God said to them, 'Be fruitful and multiply, and fill the earth and subdue it; and have dominion over the fish of the sea and over the birds of the air and over every living thing that moves upon the earth.'

God said, 'See, I have given you every plant yielding seed that is upon the face of the earth, and every tree with seed in its fruit; you shall have them for food. And to every beast of the earth, and to every bird of the air, and to everything that creeps on the earth, I have given every green plant for food.' And it was so.

—*Genesis 1:27–30*

No absolute dominion

One cannot use with impunity the different categories of beings whether living or inanimate – animals, plants, the natural elements – simply as one wishes, according to one's own economic needs. On the contrary, one must take into account the nature of each being and of its mutual connection in an ordered system which precisely is the cosmos ... Natural resources are limited; some are not renewable. Using them as if they were inexhaustible, with absolute dominion, seriously endangers their availability, not only for the present generation, but, above all, for generations to come ... We all know that the direct or indirect result of industrialisation is ever more frequently the pollution of the environment with serious consequences for the health of the population ... The dominion granted to man by the Creator is not an absolute power, nor can one speak of a freedom to use or misuse or to dispose of things as one pleases.

—*Pope John Paul II*

The covenant with Noah

Then God said to Noah and to his sons with him, 'As for me, I am establishing my covenant with you and your descendants after you, and with every living creature that is with you, as many as came out of the ark. I will establish my covenant with you, that never again shall all flesh be cut off by the waters of a flood, and never again shall there be a flood to destroy the earth.' God said, 'This is the sign of the covenant that I make between you and every living creature that is with you, for all future generations: I have set my bow in the clouds, and it shall be a sign of the covenant between me and the earth. When I bring clouds over the earth, and the bow is seen in the clouds, I will remember my covenant that is between me and you and every living creature of all flesh that is on the earth.'

—*Gen.9:8–16*

Limits to self-interest

When you come upon your enemy's ox or donkey going astray, you shall bring it back. When you see the donkey of one who hates you lying under its burden and you would hold back from setting it free, you must help to set it free. You shall not pervert the justice due to your poor in their lawsuits. Keep far from a false charge, and do not kill the innocent or those in the right, for I will not acquit the guilty. You shall take no bribe, for a bribe blinds the officials, and subverts the cause of those who are in the right. You shall not oppress the resident alien; you know the heart of an alien, for you were aliens in the land of Egypt. For six years you shall sow your land and gather in its yield; but the seventh year you shall let it rest and lie fallow; so that the poor of your people may eat; and what they leave, the wild animals may eat. You shall do the same with your vineyard and with your olive orchard. For six days you shall do your work, but on the seventh day you shall rest, so that your ox and your donkey may have relief, and your home-born slave and the resident alien may be refreshed.

—*Exodus 23:4–12*

Balaam's donkey

Balak was king of Moab. He sent messengers to Balaam son of Beor to summon him, saying, 'A people has come out of Egypt; they have spread over the face of the earth, and they have settled next to me. Come now and curse this people for me, since they are stronger than I.' God said to Balaam, 'You shall not go with them; you shall not curse the people, for they are blessed.' So Balaam rose in the morning and said to the officials of Balak, 'Go to your own land, for the Lord has refused to let me go with you.' Once again Balak sent officials and more distinguished than these. They came to Balaam and said, 'Thus says Balak son of Zippor: "Do not let anything hinder you from coming to me; for I will surely do you great honour."' But

Balaam replied, 'Although Balak were to give me his house full of silver and gold, I could not go beyond the command of the Lord my God.' That night God came to Balaam and said to him, 'If the men have come to summon you, get up and go with them; but only do what I tell you to do.'

So Balaam got up in the morning, saddled his donkey and went with the officials of Moab. God's anger was kindled because he was going, and the angel of the Lord took his stand in the road as his adversary. The donkey saw the angel standing in the road, with a drawn sword in his hand; so the donkey turned off the road and went into the field; and Balaam struck the donkey to turn it back on to the road. Then the angel stood in a narrow path between the vineyards, with a wall on either side. When the donkey saw the angel, it scraped against the wall, and scraped Balaam's foot against the wall; so that he struck it again. Then the angel stood in a narrow place, where there was no way either to the right or to the left. When the donkey saw the angel of the Lord, it lay down under Balaam; and Balaam's anger was kindled, and he struck the donkey with his staff.

Then the Lord opened the mouth of the donkey, and it said to Balaam, 'What have I done to you, that you have struck me these three times?' Balaam said to the donkey, 'Because you have made a fool of me! I wish I had a sword in my hand! I would kill you right now!' But the donkey said to Balaam, 'Am I not your donkey, which you have ridden all your life to this day? Have I been in the habit of treating you this way?' And he said, 'No.' Then the Lord opened the eyes of Balaam, and he saw the angel of the Lord standing in the road, with his drawn sword in his hands; and he bowed down, falling on his face. The angel of the Lord said to him, 'Why have you struck your donkey these three times? If it had not turned away from me, surely I would by now have killed you and let it live. Then Balaam said to the angel, 'I have sinned, for I did not know that you were standing in the road to oppose me.'

—*Numbers 22:4–34 (abridged)*

Solomon

God gave to Solomon very great wisdom, discernment and breadth of understanding as vast as the sand on the seashore, so that Solomon's wisdom surpassed the wisdom of all the people of the east, and all the wisdom of Egypt. He was wiser than anyone else … He composed three thousand proverbs, and his songs numbered a thousand and five. He would speak of trees, from the cedar that is in Lebanon to the hyssop that grows in the wall; he would speak of animals and birds, and reptiles and fish. People came from all the nations to hear the wisdom of Solomon; they came from all the kings of the earth who had heard of his wisdom.

—*1 Kings 4:29–34*

Other lives

Can you hunt the prey for the lion
or satisfy the appetite of the young lions,
when they crouch in their dens,
or lie in wait in their covert?
Who provides for the raven its prey,
when its young ones cry to God,
and wander about for lack of food?

Do you know when the mountain goats give birth?
Do you observe the calving of the deer?
Can you number the months they fulfil
and do you know the time when they give birth
when they crouch to give birth to their offspring
and are delivered of their young?
Their young ones become strong,

they grow up in the open;
they go forth and do not return to them.

Who has let the wild ass go free?
Who has loosed the bonds of the swift ass,
to which I have given the steppe for its home,
the salt land for its dwelling place?
It scorns the tumult of the city;
it does not hear the shouts of the driver.
It ranges the mountains as its pasture
and it searches after every green thing.

—Job 38:39–41; 39:1–8.

An eilid

Bha Peadail is Pòl a'dol seachad
is eilid 's an ro a' cur laoigh;
'Tha eilidh a'breith,' osa Peadail;
'Chì mi gu bheil,' osa Pòl.

'Mar a thuiteas a duille bho'n chraoibh,
gun ann an thuiteadh a seile gu làr,
an ainm Athar an àigh agus Mhic an aoibh,
agus Spiorad a' ghliocais ghràidh;
an ainm Athar an àigh agus Mhic an aoibh,
agus Spiorad a' ghliocais ghràidh.'

The hind

Peter and Paul were going along
and a hind was giving birth to a fawn
'A hind is giving birth,' said Peter
'So I see,' said Paul.

'As leaves fall from the tree,
so may her placenta fall to the ground,
in the name of the Father of joy
the Son of gladness
and the Spirit of wisdom and love;
in the name of the Father of joy
the Son of gladness
and the Spirit of wisdom and love.'

—*Anon. Hebridean*

The sacrifice of thanksgiving

Hear, O my people, and I will speak,
O Israel, I will testify against you.
I am God, your God.
Not for your sacrifices do I rebuke you;
your burnt offerings are continually before me.
I will not accept a bull from your house,
or goats from your folds.
For every wild animal of the forest is mine,
the cattle on a thousand hills.
I know all the birds of the air,
and all that moves in the field is mine.
If I were hungry, I would not tell you,
for the world and all that is in it is mine.
Do I eat the flesh of bulls,
or drink the blood of goats?
Offer to God a sacrifice of thanksgiving,
and pay your vows to the Most High.
Call on me in the day of trouble;
I will deliver you, and you shall glorify me.

—Psalm 50:115

Elijah

Elijah went a day's journey into the wilderness, and came and sat under a solitary broom tree. He asked that he might die: 'It is enough; now, O Lord, take away my life, for I am no better than my ancestors.' Then he lay down under the broom tree and fell asleep. Suddenly, an angel touched him and said to him, 'Get up and eat.' He looked, and there at his head was a cake baked on hot stones, and a jar of water. He ate and drank, and lay down again. The angel of the Lord came a second time, touched him and said to him, 'Get up and eat, otherwise the journey will be too much for you.' He got up, and ate and drank; then he went in the strength of that food for forty days and forty nights to Horeb the mount of God. At that place he came to a cave, and spent the night there.

Then the word of the Lord came to him, saying, 'What are you doing here, Elijah?' He answered, 'I have been very zealous for the Lord, the God of hosts; for the Israelites have forsaken your covenant, thrown down your altars, and killed your prophets with the sword. I alone am left, and they are seeking my life, to take it away.'

He said, 'Go out and stand on the mountain before the Lord, for the Lord is about to pass by.' Now there was a great wind, so strong that it was splitting mountains and breaking rocks in pieces before the Lord, but the Lord was not in the wind; and after the wind, an earthquake, but the Lord was not in the earthquake; and after the earthquake, a fire, but the Lord was not in the fire; and after the fire, a sound of sheer silence. When Elijah heard it, he wrapped his face in his mantle and went out and stood at the entrance of the cave. Then there came a voice to him that said, 'What are you doing here, Elijah?'

—*1 Kings 19:4–13*

Again I saw all the oppressions that are practised under the sun. Look, the tears of the oppressed – with no one to comfort them. On the side of their oppressors there was power – with no one to comfort them.

—*Ecclesiastes 4:1*

Columba and Molua's knife

Another time, a certain brother called Molua Ua Briùin approached the saint while he was writing and said, 'Please bless this implement which I am holding.' Stretching out his holy hand a little, with the pen still in it, he made the sign of the cross over it without looking up from the book which he was copying. Now when Molua had gone away with the consecrated implement, Columba said, as an afterthought, 'What was that implement which I blessed for our brother?'

'A knife,' said Diarmait, his faithful attendant, 'for slaughtering bulls and cattle.'

'I trust in my Lord,' he replied 'that the implement I blessed will do no harm to people or animals.' These words of the saint came true that very hour. For the same brother went out beyond the enclosure of the monastery intending to kill a bullock. Three times he tried, pressing hard, but he could not pierce the skin. So the skilful monks melted down that iron knife and coated all the metal implements in the monastery with it; and after that none of these could do any harm, since the saint's blessing remained on them so strongly.

—*Adomnán of Iona*

The wolf, the lamb and the holy one of God

A shoot shall come out from the stock of Jesse and a branch shall grow out of his roots. The spirit of the Lord shall rest on him, the spirit of wisdom and understanding, the spirit of counsel and might, the spirit of knowledge and the fear of the Lord ...

The wolf shall live with the lamb. The leopard shall lie down with the kid, the calf and the lion and the fatling together, and a little child shall lead them. The cow and the bear shall graze. Their young shall lie down together and the lion shall eat straw like the ox. The nursing child shall play over the hole of the asp and the weaned child shall put its hand on the adder's den. They will not hurt or destroy on all my holy mountain, for the earth will be full of the knowledge of the Lord as the waters cover the sea.

—*Isaiah 11:1–2, 6–9*

The river of the water of life

The man brought me back to the entrance of the Temple. Water was coming out from under the entrance and flowing east, the direction the Temple faced. It was flowing down from under the south part of the Temple past the south side of the altar. The man then took me out of the Temple area by way of the north gate and led me round to the gate that faces east. A small stream was flowing out at the south side of the gate. With his measuring rod, the man measured five hundred metres downstream to the east and told me to wade through the stream there. The water came only to my ankles. Then he measured another five hundred metres, and the water was up to my waist. He measured five hundred metres more, and there the stream was so deep that I could not wade through it. It was too deep to cross except by swimming. He said to me, 'Mortal man, note all this carefully.'

Then the man took me to the bank of the river, and when I got there I saw that there were very many trees on each bank. He said to me, 'This water flows through the land to the east and down into the Jordan Valley and to the Dead Sea. When it flows into the Dead Sea, it replaces the salt water of that sea with fresh water. Wherever the stream flows, there will be all kinds of animals and fish. The stream will make even the water of the Dead Sea fresh, and wherever it flows, it will bring life. From the Springs of Engedi all the way to the Springs of Eneglaim, there will be fishermen on the shore of the sea, and they will spread out their nets there to dry. There will be as many different kinds of fish as there are in the Mediterranean Sea. But the water in the marshes and ponds will not be made fresh. They will remain there as a source of salt. On each bank of the stream all kinds of trees will grow to provide food. Their leaves will never wither, and they will never stop bearing fruit. They will have fresh fruit every month, because they are watered by the stream that flows from the Temple. The trees will provide food, and their leaves will be used for healing people.

—*Ezekiel 47:1–12*

The Word was made flesh

In the beginning was the Word, and the Word was with God, and the Word was God. He was in the beginning with God. All things came into being through him, and without him, not one thing came into being. What has come into being in him was life, and the life was the light of all people. The light shines in the darkness, and the darkness did not overcome it. There was a man sent from God, whose name was John. He came to bear witness to the light, so that all might believe through him. He himself was not the light, but he came to testify to the light. The true light, which enlightens everyone, was coming into the world.

He was in the world, and the world came into being through him; yet the world did not know him. He came to what was his own, and his own people did not accept him. But to all who received him, who believed in his name, he gave power to become children of God, who were born, not of blood or of the will of the flesh or of the will of man, but of God. And the Word became flesh and lived among us, and we have seen his glory, the glory as of a father's only son, full of grace and truth.

—John 1:1–14

God in all things, all things in God

The omnipotent and perfectly holy Word of the Father himself ... is present in all things and extends his power everywhere, illuminating all things visible and invisible, containing and enclosing them in himself; he leaves nothing deprived of his power, but gives life and protection to everything, everywhere, to each individually and to all together ... Through him and his power, fire does not fight with the cold, nor the moist with the dry; but these elements which by themselves are opposed, come together like friends and kin, give life to the visible world, and become principles of existence for bodies. By obedience to this Word of God, things on earth receive life and things in heaven subsist. Through him all the sea and the great ocean keep their movement within their proper limits, and the dry land is covered with verdure in all kinds of different plants ... there is nothing existing or created which did not come into being and subsist in him and through him, as the theologian says: *'In the beginning was the Word and the Word was with God, and the Word was God. All things were made by him, and without him nothing was made.'*

—Athanasius

Temptations

Then Jesus was led up by the Spirit into the wilderness to be tempted by the devil. He fasted for forty days and forty nights, and afterwards he was famished. The tempter came and said to him, 'If you are the Son of God, command these stones to become loaves of bread.' But he answered, 'It is written, "One does not live by bread alone, but by every word that comes from the mouth of God."'

Then the devil took him to the holy city and placed him on the pinnacle of the temple, saying to him, 'If you are the Son of God, throw yourself down; for it is written, "He will command his angels concerning you," and "On their hands they will bear you up, so that you will not dash your foot against a stone."' Jesus said to him, 'Again it is written, "Do not put the Lord your God to the test."'

Again the devil took him to a very high mountain and showed him all the kingdoms of the world and their splendour; and he said to him, 'All these will I give you, if you will fall down and worship me.' Jesus said to him, 'Away with you, Satan! For it is written, "Worship the Lord your God, and serve only him."' Then the devil left him, and suddenly angels came and waited on him.

—*Matthew 4:1–11*

Consider the lilies

Someone in the crowd said to Jesus, 'Teacher, tell my brother to divide the family inheritance with me.' But he said to him, 'Friend, who set me to be a judge or arbitrator over you?' And he said to them, 'Take care! Be on your guard against all kinds of greed; for one's life does not consist in the abundance of possessions.' ...

He said to his disciples, 'Therefore I tell you, do not worry about your life, what you will eat, or about your body, what you will wear. For life is more than food, and the body more than clothing. Consider the ravens: they neither sow nor reap, they have neither storehouse nor barn, and yet God feeds them. Of how much more value are you than the birds! And can any of you by worrying add a single hour to your span of life? If then you are not able to do so small a thing as that, why do you worry about the rest? Consider the lilies, how they grow: they neither toil nor spin; yet I tell you even Solomon in all his glory was not clothed like one of these. But if God so clothes the grass of the field, which is alive today and tomorrow is thrown into the oven, how much more will he clothe you – you of little faith!'

'And do not keep striving for what you are to eat and what you are to drink, and do not keep worrying. For it is the nations of the world that strive after all these things, and your Father knows that you need them. Instead strive for his kingdom, and these things will be given to you as well. Do not be afraid, little flock, for it is your Father's good pleasure to give you the kingdom. Sell your possessions and give alms. Make purses for yourselves that do not wear out, an unfailing treasure in heaven, where no thief comes near and no moth destroys. For where your treasure is, there your heart will be also.'

—*Luke 12:13–15, 22–34*

The communion of goods

If God's providence bestows an unfailing supply of food on the birds of the air who neither sow nor reap, we ought to realise that the reason for people's supply running short is human greed. The fruits of the earth were given to feed all without distinction and nobody can claim any particular rights. Instead, we have lost the sense of the communion of goods, rushing to turn these goods into private property.

—*St Ambrose*

Hope for creation

All of creation waits with eager longing for God to reveal his children. For creation was condemned to lose its purpose, not of its own will, but because God willed it to be so. Yet there was the hope that creation itself would one day be set free from its slavery to decay and would share the glorious freedom of the children of God. For we know that up to the present time, all of creation groans with pain, like the pain of childbirth. But it is not creation alone which groans. We who have the Spirit as the first of God's gifts also groan within ourselves, as we wait for God to make us his children and set our whole being free. For it was by hope that we were saved; but if we see what we hope for, then it is not really hope. For which of us hopes for something we see? But if we hope for what we do not see, we wait for it with patience.

—*Romans 8:19–25*

Being in God

The God who made the world and everything in it, he who is Lord of heaven and earth, does not live in shrines made by human hands, nor is he served by human hands, as though he needed anything, since he himself gives to all mortals life and breath and all things. From one ancestor he made all nations to inhabit the whole earth, and he allotted the times of their existence and the boundaries of the places where they would live, so that they would search for God and perhaps grope for him and find him – though indeed he is not far from each one of us. For 'in him we live and move and have our being', even as some of your own poets have said, 'for we too are his offspring.'

—*Acts 17:24–28.*

All the world arose with him

Every material and every element and every nature which is seen in the world were all combined in the body in which Christ arose, that is in the body of every human person. Firstly there is the matter of wind and air. This is how respiration came about in human bodies. Then there is the matter of heat and boiling from fire. That is what makes the red heat of blood in bodies. Then there is the matter of the sun and the other stars of heaven, and this is what makes the lustre and light in people's eyes. Then there is the matter of bitterness and saltness; and this is what makes the bitterness of tears and the gall of the liver and much anger in human hearts. Then there is the matter of the stones and clay of the earth; and this is what joins together to form flesh and bone and limbs in human beings. Then there is the matter of the flowers and beautiful colours of earth; and this is what makes the different complexions and whiteness of faces and colour in cheeks.

All the world arose with him, for the nature of all the elements was in the body which Jesus assumed. For unless the Lord had suffered on behalf of Adam's race, and unless he had risen after death, the whole world, together with Adam's race, would be destroyed at the coming of doom; and no creature of sea or of land would be reborn, but the heavens, as far as the third heaven, would blaze. None would remain unburnt except for the three heavens of the great Heavenly Kingdom. There would be neither earth nor kindred, alive or dead, in the world, only hell and heaven, had not the Lord come to ransom them all. All would have perished in this way without renewal.

—Anon. Irish

Will animals be immortal?

'Yet there was the hope that creation itself would one day be set free from its slavery to decay and would share the glorious freedom of the children of God.' Paul does not mean that all creatures will be partakers of the same glory with the children of God, but that they will share in their own manner in the better state, because God will restore the present fallen world to perfect condition at the same time as the human race. It is neither expedient nor right for us to inquire with greater curiosity into the perfection which will be evidenced by beasts, plants, and metals, because the main part of corruption is decay. Some shrewd but unbalanced commentators ask whether all kinds of animals will be immortal. If we give free reign to these speculations, where will they finally carry us? Let us therefore be content with this simple doctrine – their constitution will be such, and their order so complete, that no appearance either of deformity or of impermanence will be seen.

—John Calvin

WISE & FOOLISH NOTIONS

Ag iasgach a' mhic-meanmna

Air madainn Samhna,
a'tighinn tarsainn Bràgh na Teanga,
chunna mi tràlair a-muigh sa Chuan Sgìth.

Ring-netters m'eachainn,
sgadan drithleannach mo chuimhne,
agus an cuan cho mòr, 's cho àlainn, 's cho farsaing.

Stad mi mionaid
aig Bealach an t-Sliachd
a'cur lìon tharis mo smuaintean.

An sluagh air glùinean,
an Eaglais,
agus an cuan domhainn gar cuartachadh.

Fishing the imagination

On a November morning
coming over Upper Teangue,
I saw a trawler out in the Minch.

The ring-netters of my mind,
the glittering herring of my memory,
and the ocean so big, and so beautiful, and so wide.

I stopped for a moment
at the Brae of Humility
flinging a net over my thoughts.

The people on their knees,
the Church,
and the deep sea surrounding us.

—*Angus Peter Campbell*

Patrick and the daughters of Loiguire

Then St Patrick came to a well called Clebach on the eastern slopes of Cruachu before sunrise and they sat down by the well; and behold two daughters of King Loiguire, fair-haired Ethne and red-haired Fedelm, came to the well to wash in the morning as women do, and they found Patrick by the well with his assembly of holy bishops. And they did not know who they were nor their appearance or what tribe or country they came from, but they thought they might be men from the fairy-mounds or earth gods or an apparition; and the girls said to them: 'Where is your home and where do you come from?' and Patrick said to them: 'It would be better for you to recognise our true God than to ask about our people.'

The first girl said: 'Who is god and where is god and whose god is he and where is his dwelling? Does your god have sons and daughters, gold and silver? Does he live for ever, is he handsome, has his son been fostered by many, are his daughters dear and beautiful to the men of this world? Is he in heaven or on earth, in water, in the rivers, mountains or valleys? Tell us about him, how he may be seen, how he may be loved, how he may be found, whether in youth or in old age.'

Then St Patrick, filled with the Holy Spirit said: 'Our God is the God of all people, God of heaven and earth, the sea and rivers, God of the sun and the moon and all the stars, God of high mountains and low valleys; God above heaven and in heaven and under heaven; he has his dwelling in heaven and earth and the sea and in all that is in them; he breathes in everything, makes all things live, is beyond everything, supports everything; he lights up the light of the sun, he maintains the light of the night and of the stars; and he made springs and dry land and dry islands in the sea, and stars to serve the great lights. He has a Son who is co-eternal with him, similar to him; the Son is not younger than the Father nor the Father older, and the Holy Spirit breathes in them; Father, Son and Holy Spirit are inseparable. Now truly, I want to unite you with the heavenly king, since you are daughters of an earthly king, if you are able to believe. And the girls said, as with one voice and heart, 'Teach us most diligently how we may believe in the heavenly king, so that we can see him face to face. Tell us, and we will do as you say.'

—*Tírechán*

Beware soul brother

We are the men of soul
men of song we measure out
our joys and agonies
too, our long, long passion week
in paces of the dance. We have
come to know from surfeit of suffering
that even the Cross need not be
a dead end nor total loss
if we should go to it striding
the dirge of the soulful abia drums …

But beware soul brother
of the lures of ascension day
the day of soporific levitation
on high winds of skysong; beware
for others there will be that day
lying in wait leaden-footed, tone-deaf
passionate only for the deep entrails
of our soil; beware of the day
we head truly skyward leaving
that spoil to the long ravenous tooth
and talon of their hunger.
Our ancestors, soul brother, were wiser
than is often made out. Remember
they gave Ala, great goddess
of their earth, sovereignty too over
their arts for they understood
too well those hard-headed

men of departed dance where a man's
foot must return whatever beauties
it may weave in air, where
it must return for safety
and renewal of strength. Take care
then, mother's son, lest you become
a dancer disinherited in mid-dance
hanging a lame foot in air like the hen
in a strange unfamiliar compound. Pray
protect this patrimony to which
you must return when the song
is finished and the dancers disperse;
for they in their time will want
a place for their feet when
they come of age and the dance
of the future is born
for them.

—*Chinua Achebe*

Lost

To quote my distant friend Imran MacLeod,
'A man with no culture has no identity.'

The last I heard from him, he was off
To the Himalayas.

He had a very confused childhood.

Father was Scottish,
Mother Pakistani.

They'd always be arguing over many things
Concerning him.

One was religion.

Father wanted him brought up
A Catholic; mother wanted a Muslim.

Was he the only boy on our street who went
To mosque on Fridays and chapel on Sundays.

But in the mountains

God's sure to find him.

—*Hamid Shami*

24,000 feet

Here we are, Abba,
twenty-four-thousand feet,
the plane is full,
your sunshine fills the cabin.

You know
where we have been
and why.

The businessman with the Hamleys bag,
the sleeping grandmother,
the party in red and white scarves,
the bare-legged girls,
two women in salwar kamiz,
children, students, frequent flyers
neatly stowed, their gloved
fingers flicking: headlines,
foreign news, financial pages

Behind us
hundreds of gallons of burnt fuel
fall to earth,
drift heavenwards

Who can untangle this?
Africa dying,
cities buried in mud.

    —Lucy Menezies

The treatment of the Earth by man the exploiter is not only imprudent, it is sacrilegious. We are not likely to correct our hideous mistakes in this realm unless we recover the mystical sense of our oneness with nature. Many people think this is fantastic. I think it is fundamental to our sanity.

—*William Temple*

Disconnected souls

We ourselves are part of the earth we know, as old as the earth itself, and know from the memory of nature that is innate in us, nature's language without being taught. Nature is the mirror in which the soul sees itself. Even in our cities there is day and night and rain and wind and trees, fountains in our public parks, flower-beds of all sorts. We cannot live without these things because they tell us and remind us continually of what we are. We lived for millennia as children of the earth before we built our cities and those modern industrial 'inner city areas' whose severance from the natural world is an outrage to the souls of their inhabitants, whether they know it or not. To be severed from nature and from all those images that remind us of who we are causes sorrow – depression it is called nowadays – and violence. Our very humanity is threatened as the machine – an idol built in the likeness of an ideology – takes control of human lives. The rich buy weekend cottages to 'get away from it all'. The poor buy package holidays just to sit by the sea and watch the ebb and flow of the waves and to feel the light and heat of the sun, for these are the very language of life. Even one leaf, one flower of the green living earth can heal the mind and heart as no synthetic object ever can.

—*Kathleen Raine*

You haven't a hope unless ...

Politically, the world is too far gone. It is not a question of nearing the abyss. We daily look down into it if we choose to open our eyes, and millions are already at the bottom of it. To that extent, politics merely legitimises callousness, unapologetic self-interest and the kind of cynicism which has so far escaped the Green Movement. Do not turn away from that dark side. It is there in each and every one of us ...

I pretend, of course, to be impressed by the artistic excellence of the adverts that I see on television, but deep down, I can feel those little psychological hooks reaching out, trying to pull me down. And if that's true of fully paid-up Greens, how do we think we're going to impress others? Despite all the hard-working Green campaigners, the hydra-headed monster of industrialism has, frankly, slipped its leash. We will not tame it again. It is not so much decapitation that we should be aiming for, as the decommissioning of the entire monster.

From some perspectives (which I consider to be realistic but by no means apocalyptic) I remain fairly astonished that so many people in the Green Movement still suppose that our job can be achieved by *political* means alone. They suppose it still, after so many years of confronting the gap between what we wish to achieve politically and knowing full well what we actually can achieve in time.

I remember some years ago, at the Second International Green Congress in Dover, the Bishop of Lewes, Father Peter, opening the proceedings by pitching a message that many found hard to accept. What he said was: 'I must say this to you: you haven't a hope in a million years of changing anything by political methods unless you concentrate on changing attitudes, changing thought-forms deep, deep down in society, or at least understanding the need to do this.'

—*Jonathon Porritt*

Melangell's sanctuary

In Powys there was once a certain most illustrious prince by the name of Brychwel Ysgithrog, who was the Earl of Chester and who at that time lived in the town of Pengwern Powys, which means in Latin the head of Powys marsh… When one day, in the year of our Lord 604, the said prince had gone hunting to a certain place in Britain called Pennant, in the said principality of Powys, and when the hunting dogs of the same prince had started a hare, the dogs pursued the hare and he too gave chase until he came to a certain thicket of brambles, which was large and full of thorns. In this thicket he found a girl of beautiful appearance who, given up to divine contemplation, was praying with the greatest devotion, with the said hare lying boldly and fearlessly under the hem or fold of her garments, its face towards the dogs.

Then the prince cried, 'Get it, hounds, get it!' but the more he shouted, urging them on, the further the dogs retreated and fled, howling, from the little animal. Finally the prince, altogether astonished, asked the girl how long she had lived on her own on his lands, in such a lonely spot. In reply the girl said that she had not seen a human face for these fifteen years. Then he asked the girl who she was, her place of birth and origins, and in all humility she answered that she was the daughter of King Jowchel of Ireland and that 'because my father had intended me to be the wife of a certain great and generous Irishman, I fled from my native soil and under the guidance of God came here in order that I might serve God and the immaculate Virgin with my heart and pure body until my dying day'.

Then the prince asked the girl her name. She replied that her name was Melangell. Then the prince, considering in his innermost heart the flourishing though solitary state of the girl, said, 'O most worthy virgin Melangell, I find that you are a handmaid of the true God and most sincere follower of Christ. Therefore because it has pleased the highest and all-powerful God to give refuge, for your merits, to this little wild hare with safe conduct and protection from the attack and pursuit of these savage and violent dogs, I give and present you most willingly these my lands for the service of God, that they may be a perpetual asylum, refuge and defence, in honour of your name, excellent girl. Let neither king nor prince seek to be so rash or bold towards God that they presume to drag away any man or woman who has escaped here, desiring to enjoy protection in these your lands, as long as they in no way contaminate or pollute your sanctuary or asylum.

This virgin Melangell, who was so very pleasing to God, led her solitary life, as stated above, for thirty seven years in this very same place. And the hares, which are little wild creatures, surrounded her every day of her life just as if they had been tame or domesticated animals.

—Anon. Welsh

Outrageous demands

But is all of this Christian?... Is it commensurate with the radical, destabil- ising, inclusive love of Jesus? It appears to be, for Jesus is reputed to have made the classic subject-subject statement when he said 'Love your enemies'. Treat the person who is against you, perhaps even out to kill you, as a subject, as someone deserving respect and care, as the Good Samaritan treated his enemy in need. If Jesus could say, 'Love your enemies', surely he would find the much milder statement, 'Love nature', perfectly acceptable. If enemies are to be shown respect and care, should not other lifeforms also, as well as the habitats which support them? Loving nature this way, not with mushy feeling or charity but with respect for its otherness, its Thouness, and with a desire to care for it, will not be easy. But loving other humans, especially enemies, is not either. Chris- tianity is not an easy religion. As counter-cultural, it will make outrageous demands, like 'Love your enemies' and 'Love nature'.

—*Sallie McFague*

Gliocas a lorg / Finding wisdom

Gliocas a lorg – chan e sin an duilgheadas. Sann ann an gliocas
a tha sinn beò 's a' gluasad 's a tha ar bith againn.
Se tha duilich ùmhlachd a thoirt dhan Ghliocas a tha sinn air lorg.

Finding wisdom – that's not the problem. It's in wisdom
that we live and move and exist.
The problem is submitting to the wisdom we have found.

—*Fearghas MacFhionnlaigh*

Casan Sìoda

Air tilleadh dhachaidh feasgar dhomh 's an teine ag cur ruaim dheth
chunnaic mi an creachadair 'na laighe socair suaimhneach;
cha n-fhaicinn ach an druim dheth, fionnadh dubh is bàrr a chluasan –
fhuair mi Casan Sìoda 'na shìneadh anns an luaithre.

"Sud thusa 'na do chuachaig gun smuain air làmh do bhiathaidh,
'nad stidean leisg mì-thaingeil, làn aingidheachd is mialaich;
b'olc gu leòir 'nad phiseag thu, droch stic nam prat mi-rianail,
ach nis is làn-chat feusaig thu a réir na chaill mi dh'iasg leat.

Sealgair nan trannsa is fear-rannsachaidh nan cùiltean,
Ord nan Luch 'gan tòireachd le do chròcan, 's cha b'e 'n sùgradh;
Freiceadan Dubh gach tollaig is tu roimpe 'na do chrùban,
ceatharnach sa' chistin nì na measraichean a sgrùdadh.

'S e Spògan Sròil a b'athair dhuit, fear caithreamach na h-oidhche,
a fhuair ri Coiseachd Chlùimh thu, bean chiùin a b'fhaide ìghnean;
fhuair thu do thogail ris a'ghoid, 's cha b'ann gu dìomhain –
's nach olc an sgoil a thug iad dhuit, a mhurtair nan eun bìdeach?

Chan eil gealbhonn no smeòrach o Ghleann Crò gu ruig Loch Fìne,
lon-dubh no gobhlan-gaoithe o Ard Laoigh gu Gleann Sìora,
chan eil eireag bheag no luchag no eun-guir am preas 'san rìoghachd
nach eil air fhaicill roimh do spògan – ochòin, a Chasan Sìoda!

Seachain an cù aosda le a chraos 's a shùilean gruamach,
thugad bean na còcaireachd 's a'phoit 'na làimh gu bualadh,
seachain an cat buidhe ud, laoch guineach air leth-chluais e,
No bheir e Inbhir Lòchaidh dhuit, mo Spògan Sìoda uallach!

So rabhadh dhuit, a mhic ud, is na leigear e an dìochuimhn'
nuair thig mi dhachaidh anmoch lethmharbh 's air mo mhìobhadh
ma gheibh mi 'na mo chathair thu, o seallaidh mi le cinnt dhuit
nach *persona grata* thu, a ghràidh, a Chasan Sìoda."

Silk Feet

Coming home in the evening, when the fire was throwing out
  a ruddy glow,
I saw the plunderer lying peacefully at his ease;
I could only see his back, black fur, the tips of his ears –
I found Silk Feet reposing on the ashes.

'There you are coiled up without a thought for the hand that feeds you
a bad ungrateful pussy full of ungodliness and meowing;
You were bad enough when a kitten, a bad stick full of disorderly pranks
but now you are a full-grown whiskered cat, judging by the amount of fish
I have lost through you.'

'Huntsman of the lobbies and investigator of the nooks and crannies
Hammer of the Mice, pursuing them with your grappling hooks
and it's no joking matter
Black Watch of every chink, crouching before it;
cateran in the kitchen who will scrutinise the dishes.'

'Satin Paws was your father, the loud musician of the night;
he had you by Downy Tread, a gentle lady, with claws of the longest;
You were brought up on thieving, and not idly –
and wasn't it a bad education they gave you, murderer of the tiny birds?'

'There's not a sparrow or a thrush from Glen Croe to Loch Fyne
a blackbird or a swallow from Ardlui to Glen Shira
there's not a little chicken or a mouse or a broodie bird in any bush
in the kingdom
but it's on its guard against your paws. Alas, Silk Feet.'

'Avoid the aged dog with his maw and his glum eyes;
look out for the cook with the pot in her hand to hit you;
avoid yon yellow cat – he's a ferocious warrior with one ear –
or he'll give you an Inverlochy, my jaunty Silk Paws.'

'Here's a warning for you, you son of a devil, and don't let it be forgotten.
When I come home late, half dead and battered by the weather
if I find you in my chair, oh, I will show you quite decidedly
that you are not *persona grata*, my darling Silk Feet.'

—*George Campbell Hay*

Isaac the Syrian

'What is a charitable heart?' asks St Isaac the Syrian – 'It is a heart which is burning with charity for the whole of creation, for people, for the birds, for the beasts, for the demons – for all creatures. Those who have such a heart cannot see or call to mind a creature, without their eyes becoming filled with tears by reason of the immense compassion which seizes their heart; a heart which is softened and can no longer bear to see or learn from others of any suffering, even the smallest pain, being inflicted upon a creature. This is why such a person never ceases to pray also for the animals, for the enemies of Truth and for those who do him evil, that they be pre-served and purified. He will pray even for the reptiles, moved by the infi-nite pity which reigns in the hearts of those who are becoming united to God.' In his way to union with God, a man in no way leaves creatures aside, but gathers together in his love the whole cosmos disordered by sin, that it may at last be transfigured by grace.

—*Vladimir Lossky*

Love is ...

Love is the extremely difficult realisation that something other than oneself is real. Love ... is the discovery of reality.

—*Iris Murdoch*

What the butcher said

A little while ago, I met on the road a butcher returning to Tula after a visit to his home. He is not yet an experienced butcher and his duty is to stab with a knife. I asked him whether he did not feel sorry for the animals that he killed. He gave me the usual answer: 'Why should I feel sorry? It is necessary.' But when I told him that eating flesh was not necessary, but is only a luxury, he agreed; and then he admitted that he was sorry for the animals. 'But what can I do?' he said, 'I must earn my bread. At first I was afraid to kill. My father, he never killed a chicken in all his life.' The majority of Russians cannot kill; they feel pity, and express the feeling by the word 'fear'. This man had also been 'afraid', but he was so no longer. He told me that most of the work was done on Fridays, when it continues until the evening. Not long ago, I also had a talk with a retired soldier, a butcher, and he too was surprised at my assertion that it was a pity to kill, and said the usual things about its being ordained. But afterwards he agreed with me: 'Especially when they are quiet, tame cattle. They come, poor things! Trusting you. It is very pitiful.' This is dreadful! Not the suffering and death of the animals, but that man suppresses in himself, unnecessarily, the highest spiritual capacity – that of sympathy and pity towards living creatures like himself – and by violating his own feelings becomes cruel.

—*Leo Tolstoy*

Cruel nature and reverence for life

Reverence for life and sympathy with other lives is of supreme importance for this world of ours. Nature has no similar reverence for life. It produces life a thousandfold in the most meaningful way and destroys it a thousandfold in the most meaningless way. In every stage of life, right up to the level of human beings, terrible ignorance lies over all creatures. They have the will to live but no capacity for compassion toward other creatures ... Nature looks beautiful and marvellous when you view it from the outside. But when you read its pages like a book, it is horrible. And its cruelty is so senseless. The most precious form of life is sacrificed to the lowliest. A child breathes the germs of tuberculosis. He grows and flourishes but is destined to suffering and a premature death because these lowly creatures multiply in his vital organs ...

This, then, is the enigmatic contradiction in the will to live – life against life, causing suffering and death, innocent and yet guilty. Nature teaches cruel egotism, only briefly interrupted by the urge it has planted in creatures to offer love and assistance for their offspring as long as necessary. Animals love their young so much that they are willing to die for them. They have this capacity for sympathy. Yet the self-perpetuation of the species makes all the more terrible their utter lack of concern for those beings unrelated to them. The world given over to ignorance and egotism is like a valley shrouded in darkness. Only up on the peaks is there light. All must live in darkness.

Only one creature can escape and catch a glimpse of the light: the highest creature, humankind. We are permitted to achieve the knowledge of reverence for life ... and this understanding is the great event in the evolution of life. Through it, truth and goodness appear in the world. Light shines in the darkness. The highest form of life has been attained, life sharing the life of others, in which one existence shares the life of the whole world and life becoming aware of its all-embracing existence. Individual isolation ceases. Outside life streams like a flood into our own. We live in the world and the world lives in us.

—*Albert Schweitzer*

Yes to the Earth

So radiant in certain mornings' light
With its roses and its cypress trees
Is Earth, or with its grain and olives;

So suddenly it is radiant on the soul,
Which stands then alone and forgetful
Though just a moment earlier the soul
Wept bloody tears or dwelt in bitterness;

So radiant in certain mornings' light
Is Earth, and in its silence so expressive,
This wondrous lump rolling in its skies;
Beautiful, tragic in solitude, yet smiling,

That the soul, unasked, replies
'Yes' replies 'Yes' to the Earth,
To the indifferent Earth, 'Yes!'

Even though next instant skies
Should darken, roses too, and cypresses,
Or the effort of life grow heavier still,
The act of breathing even more heroic,
'Yes' replies the battered soul to Earth,
So radiant in the light of certain mornings
Beautiful above all things, and human hope.

—*Sibilla Aleramo*

Antiphon for the Holy Spirit

The Holy Spirit is life that gives life,
moving all things.
It is the root in every creature
and purifies all things
wiping away sins,
anointing wounds.
It is radiant life, worthy of praise
awakening and enlivening
all things

—*St Hildegard of Bingen*

The heaven of animals

Here they are. The soft eyes open.
If they have lived in a wood
It is a wood.
If they have lived on plains
It is grass rolling
Under their feet forever.

Having no souls, they have come,
Anyway, beyond their knowing.
Their instincts wholly bloom
And they rise.
The soft eyes open.

To match them, the landscape flowers,
Outdoing, desperately
Outdoing what is required:
The richest wood,
The deepest field.

For some of these,
It could not be the place
It is, without blood.
These hunt, as they have done,
But with claws and teeth grown perfect.

More deadly than they can believe.
They stalk more silently,
And crouch on the limbs of trees,
And their descent
Upon the bright backs of their prey

May take years
In a sovereign floating of joy.
And those that are hunted
Know this as their life,
Their reward: to walk

Under such trees in full knowledge
Of what is in glory above them,
And feel no fear,
But acceptance, compliance.
Fulfilling themselves, without pain.

At the cycle's centre,
They tremble, they walk
Under the tree,
They fall, they are torn,
They rise, they walk again.

—James Dickey

The bells of heaven

'Twould ring the bells of heaven,
the wildest peal for years,
if parson lost his senses
and people came to theirs
and he and they together
knelt down with angry prayers
for tamed and shabby tigers
and dancing dogs and bears
and wretched blind pit ponies
and little hunted hares

—*Ralph Hodgson*

An elegant simplicity

In our time, the pursuit of affluence has become a new religion, the religion of materialism. Acquisition of wealth has become a good thing in itself. Now, if six billion of us want to acquire the American level of living standards we will need to mine the resources of four or five planets. Unfortunately we haven't got four or five planets to be mined. We only have one planet earth and it is already under stress.

From a Buddhist perspective, while millions of our fellow humans have no food, no easy access to clean water, no homes and other basics of life, the endless pursuit of wealth is morally untenable. Especially if this degree of affluence has to be defended with enormous defence budgets including nuclear weapons …

These days, poverty has become a dirty word. It has become associated with starvation and deprivation. This was not always the case. The Buddha, Jesus Christ, St Francis and Mahatma Gandhi embraced poverty and virtues of the simple life. According to them, poverty is not the problem. Affluence is the problem. Poverty is the solution. There is enough in the world for everybody's need but not enough for anybody's greed, said Gandhi. The Shakers in America also pursued a similar path of elegant simplicity because they believed that it is a gift to be simple, it is a gift to be free. Too much wealth increases fear and curtails freedom. The moral imperative for Europe is not relentless economic growth, but to live simply so that others may simply live.

—*Satish Kumar*

Columbanus and the bear

Columbanus was weakening his body by fasting, under a cliff in the wilderness, and he had no food except the apples of the country … A fierce bear of great voracity came and began to lick off the necessary food and carry the apples away in its mouth. When the meal-time came, Columbanus directed Chagnoald, his servant, to bring the usual quantity of apples. The latter went and saw the bear wandering about among the fruit-trees and bushes and licking off the apples. He returned hastily and told the father, who commanded him to go and set aside a part of the fruit-trees for food for the bear and order it to leave the others for himself. Chagnoald went in obedience to the command, and dividing with his staff the trees and bushes which bore the apples he, in accordance with Columbanus's command, set aside the part that the bear should eat, and the other part that it should leave for the use of the man of God. Wonderful obedience of the bear! It did not venture at all to take food from the prohibited part but, as long as the man of God remained in that place, sought food only from the trees that had been assigned to it.

—*Jonas*

Cheetah, antelope, hunter

What, then, would God know and care about, say, a cheetah? Presumably God would know the whole evolutionary history of cheetahs, and the history of this particular cheetah; the cheetah's physical components of particles and molecules; its biological nature as a carnivore and its relation to other big cats; the ecological niche it occupies in the local system; its success or failure in finding food supply, in mating, and in its rearing of cubs (at least if it is a female cheetah). Such knowledge would concern both cheetahs generally and the specific happenings of this particular cheetah's life.

God knows how the world looks and smells to a cheetah. Equally the divine presence will see the grace and power of the cheetah at full stretch after prey; will know the frustration at failure and its satisfaction at a successful kill which it can keep from hyenas and other predators ... But God will also know the antelope's experience of the cheetah as predator; the local human beings' view of it; the white hunter's view of it as quarry, with all the hinterland of beliefs and practices which that implies ...

From that instance of the cheetah, one must extrapolate to all creatures great and small, wild and tame, past, present and future. Yet God's love, like God's presence, is not made thin and general by being offered to all. The divine presence and love is constant and does not admit of degrees, so they are concentrated on each individual at each time, and are as total for non-human beings as for human beings.

—*Ruth Page*

Creation and evolution

It is interesting to contemplate a tangled bank, clothed with many plants of many kinds, with birds singing on the bushes, with various insects flitting about, and with worms crawling through the damp earth, and to reflect that these elaborately constructed forms, so different from each other in so complex a manner, have all been produced by laws acting around us. These laws, taken in the largest sense, being Growth and Reproduction; Inheritance, which is almost implied by reproduction; Variability from indirect and direct action of the conditions of life, and so as a consequence to Natural Selection, entailing Divergence of Character and Extinction of less-improved forms. Thus, from the war of nature, from famine and death, the most exalted object which we are capable of conceiving, namely the production of the higher animals, directly follows. There is grandeur in this view of life, with its several powers, having been originally breathed by the Creator into a few forms or into one; and that, whilst this planet has gone cycling on according to the fixed law of gravity, from so simple a beginning endless forms most beautiful and most wonderful have been and are being evolved.

—*Charles Darwin*

Word made flesh

Word whose breath is the world-circling atmosphere,
Word that utters the world that turns the wind,
Word that articulates the bird that speeds upon the air,

Word that blazes out the trumpet of the sun,
whose silence is the violin-music of the stars,
whose melody is the dawn, and harmony the night,

Word traced in water of lakes, and light on water,
light on still water, moving water, waterfall,
and water colours of cloud, of dew, of spectral rain,

Word inscribed on stone, mountain range upon range of stone,
Word that is fire of the sun, and fire within
order of atoms, crystalline symmetry,

Grammar of five-fold rose and six-fold lily,
spiral of leaves on a bough, helix of shells,
rotation of twining plants on axes of darkness and light,

Instinctive wisdom of fish and lion and ram,
rhythm of generation in flagellate and fern,
flash of fin, beat of wing, heartbeat, beat of the dance,

Hieroglyph in whose exact precision is defined
feather and insect-wing, refraction of multiple eyes,
eyes of the creatures, oh myriad-fold vision of the world,

Statement of mystery, how shall we name
a spirit clothed in world, a world made man?

—*Kathleen Raine*

Not just for us

Although it cannot be denied that human beings are very much at the centre of biblical teaching on creation, this teaching does not hold that nature has been created simply for our sake. It exists for God's glory, that is to say, it has meaning and worth beyond its meaning and worth as seen from the point of view of human utility. It is in this sense that we can say that it has intrinsic value. To imagine that God has created the whole universe simply for our use and pleasure is a mark of folly. The wise person will be able to read lessons for human behaviour from his or her observation of nature. Although in the New Testament there enters a note of apocalyptic pessimism, it remains true that the world as God's creation is in essence good. This natural world is not corrupt in itself (as Gnostics and some others held) but is in bondage to the powers of darkness, from whose grasp it can be delivered. God has a redeeming purpose for the whole creation, for nature as well as for men and women. This, we would claim, is the teaching of the mainstream of biblical thought.

—*Anglican Bishops 1975*

A Community of creatures

I will make for you a covenant on that day with the wild animals, the birds of the air, and the creeping things of the ground; and I will abolish the bow, the sword and war from the land; and I will make you lie down in safety.

—Hosea 2:18

Here
on the white beach
with nothing in my rucksack
but an empty notebook:
'OK, we know you've studied
but what have you SEEN?'
Shoji to Hakuin –
waiting and watching

—Kenneth White

INTERCESSIONS

Call to stillness

Everything as it moves, now and then, here and there, makes pauses.

The bird, as it flies, stops in one place to make its nest, and in another to rest in its flight.

In the same way, God has paused as well.

The sun, which is so bright and beautiful, is one place where God has paused.

The moon, the stars, the winds: God has been with them, too.

The trees, the animals, are all places where God has stopped, leaving the touch of the Holy in all these things.

We too have had God pause in us. We too have the Holy touch in our beings.

Let us now pause ourselves, and listen for the voice of God in our hearts.

—Anon. Lakota

The bodhisattva

For as long as space endures
and for as long as living beings remain
until then may I too abide
to dispel the misery of the world

—*Shantideva*

For frightened animals

Hear our prayer, O God, for our friends the animals, especially for animals who are suffering; for any that are hunted or lost, or deserted or frightened or hungry; for all that must be put to death. We ask you to have mercy and pity on them all; and for those who deal with them we ask a heart of compassion and gentle words and kindly words. Make us, ourselves, to be true friends to animals and so to share the blessings of the merciful.

—*Albert Schweitzer*

My God,
through the boldness of your Revelation
explode the timorous small-minded thinking
that dares not conceive of anything greater
or more alive in this world
than the pitiful perfection
of the human organism.

—*Pierre Teilhard de Chardin*

A Border shepherd prays for a thaw

Is the whiteness of desolation to lie still
on the mountains of our land for ever?
Is the earthly hope of your servants
to perish frae the face of the earth?
The flocks on a thousand hills are thine –
and their lives or deaths wad be naething to thee –
thou wad be neither the richer nor the poorer;
but it is a great matter to us.
Have pity then, on the lives o' thy creatures,
for beast and body are a' thy handiwark,
and send us the little wee cludd out of the sea like a man's hand,
to spread and darken and pour and plash,
till the green gladsome face o' nature aince mair appear.

—*Adam Scott / James Hogg*

May 6th 1948, Ascension

Yesterday Father Macarius and I went out and blessed the fields, starting with the wheat and oats and coming round by Saint Bernard's field and Aidan Nally's and across the bottoms. Out in the calf pasture we blessed some calves who came running up and took a very active interest in every-thing. Then we blessed pigs, who showed some interest at first. The sheep showed no concern and the chickens ran away as soon as we approached. The rabbits stayed quiet until we threw holy water at them and then they all jumped.

—*Thomas Merton*

For the necessities of life

Let us pray:
For an abundance of water
in our rivers this year,
that Christ our Lord will bless them
and fill them to the brim.
May he generously increase the yield
of the land which sustains us.
May he supply our human needs,
guard our flocks and herds
and forgive us our sins.
Lord, have mercy.

Let us pray:
For the trees, the wild plants
and the cultivated ground,
that Christ, our Lord, may bless them,
that they may flourish and bring forth a rich harvest.
May he have compassion on his whole creation
and forgive us our sins.
Lord, have mercy.

Increase, O God, the fertility of the earth,
water it abundantly, for we are in your hands.
Crown the year with your goodness
for the sake of the poorest of your people,
the widow, the orphan, the stranger
and all your creatures.
We look to you, hope of our lives,
that your name may be blessed among us.
Give us our bread in due time.
Treat us, O Lord, according to your goodness,
you who give food enough for all.
Fill our hearts with joy and gratitude
so that, equipped with the necessities of life,
we may grow in every good work.
Amen.

> —Anon., based on Coptic liturgy

A dog's prayer

Lord
I keep watch
If I were not here
who would guard their house?
Who would guard their sheep?
Who would stand by them?
You and I are the only ones
who really understand
what faithfulness is.
They say 'Good dog, nice dog.'
Just words …
I accept their petting
and the old bones they throw me,
and I look pleased.
They think this makes me happy.
I accept kicks too
when they come along.
None of that matters.
My business is to watch.
Lord, let me not die
till all danger
has been driven from their door.
Amen.

—*Carmen Bernos de Gasztold*

Animals

Dear Lord,
Thank you for animals.
Sometimes when we are lonely, animals can comfort us.
Animals are wonderful and need lots of love and care.
Help people who treat animals badly
to see what they are doing to your creatures.

—Christopher Thomaidis, age 11

Beannachd iasgaich

Ta na soillse thàinig oirnn,
rugadh Crìosda leis an Oigh.

'Na ainm-san cratham am bùrn
air gach càil a ta na m'chùrt.

A Rìgh nam feart 's nan neart tha shuas,
do bheannachd iasgaich dòrt a nuas.

Suidhim sìos le ràmh 'na m'ghlac,
imirim a seachd ceud 's a seachd.

Tilgidh mi mo dhubhan sìos
's an ciad iasg a bheir mi nìos,

An ainm Chrìosda, Rìgh nan sian,
gheobh an deòir e mar a mhiann

Is rìgh nan iasgair, Peadair treun,
bheir e bheannachd dhomh na dhèigh.

Airil, Gabril agus Eòin
Raphail bàigheil, agus Pòl,

Calum-cille caomh 's gach càs,
's Muire mhìn-gheal leis a ghràs.

Siùbhlaibh leinn gu iola cuain
ciùinibh dhuinne bàrr nan stuagh.

Righ nan rìgh ri crìch ar cuart
sineadh saoghail is sonais buan.

Crùn an Rìgh o'n Trì tha shuas
Crois Chrìosda d'ar dìon a nuas.

Crùn an Rìgh o'n Trì tha shuas
Crois Chrìosda d'ar dìon a nuas.

Fishing blessing

The light has dawned on us
Christ is born of the Virgin.

In his name I sprinkle water
on everything around me.

Oh King of deeds and powers above
pour down your blessing on our fishing.

I will sit down and take hold of an oar.
I will row seven hundred and seven strokes.

I will cast my hook over the side
and the first fish that I bring up

The poor shall have their fill of it
in the name of Christ, King of the Elements.

And bold Peter, king of fishermen
will bless me for it afterwards.

Ariel, Gabriel and John,
merciful Raphael and Paul

Columba, kindly in every hardship
and sweet fair Mary, full of grace

Come with us to the fishing bank on the ocean
calm the crest of the waves for us

King of kings at our journey's end
long life and lasting happiness

The King's crown from the Three above
the Cross of Christ to protect us below

The King's crown from the Three above
the Cross of Christ to protect us below

—Anon. Hebridean

Bean an iasgair

Cha d'fhuair mi'n cadal fad na h-oidhche,
    o dhubh gu soillse 's mi faisg air gul:
a'ghaoth cho sgalail is mi ga h-èisdeachd,
    is m'fhear fhèin is an sgoth a-muigh.

Bha mi a'guidhe dìon is fasgaidh
    on ghaillinn dhorcha don sgoth dhuinn,
eadar Arainn is bàghan Chòmhail.
    Is mairg dom beòshlaint lìon is muir.

Buidseach na foille 's an aodainn phreasaich,
    àilleag nan geas 's nan ceudan cruth,
brù às an d'èirich rèidhlean 's garbhlach –
    dubh fhairge nan stuadh 's nan sruth.

The fisherman's wife

I got no sleep all the night
from dark to daylight, and I near crying:
the wind so shrill and I listening to it
and my own man and the skiff out at sea.

I was praying for shielding and shelter
from the dark gale for the brown skiff
between Arran and the bays of Cowal.
Unlucky is he whose livelihood is a net and the sea.

Treacherous witch of the wrinkled face,
bonny enchantress of the hundreds of shifting shapes
womb from which arose both plain and rough mountain land –
wretched sea of the waves and the tides.

    —*George Campbell Hay*

The other

There are nights that are so still
that I can hear the small owl calling
far off and a fox barking
miles away. It is then that I lie
in the lean hours awake and listening
to the swell born somewhere in the Atlantic
rising and falling, rising and falling
wave on wave on the long shore
by the village, that is without light
and companionless. And the thought comes
of that other being who is awake, too.
Letting our prayers break on him,
not like this for a few hours,
but for days, years, for eternity.

—R.S. Thomas

War

Hello God,
can you hear me
above all the noise?
It's us fighting one another.
Please help us to stop all our wars.
Amen.

—Josephine Davies, age 9

Women's tree-planting prayer

Lord, we ask you to bless
the Women's Club at Wadzanai Doroguru …
You have allowed us to plant trees and vegetables
as you have planted in your own garden, Eden
where you allowed your representatives to live.
We thank you that you have reintroduced that privilege for us women,
we, the stewards of your creation.
We thank you for male support,
for the good men who have dug holes for our trees.
Bless the people of ZIRRCON whom you have sent here.
Bless them as they traverse all of Zimbabwe to plant trees.
Mwari, let this task have your full endorsement …
Strengthen us in our earth-keeping quest
and let the message within the sermons keep motivating us.
Amen.

—Association of African Earth-keeping Churches

God bless the grass that grows through the crack,
they roll the concrete over it to try and keep it back.
The concrete gets tired of what it has to do,
it breaks and it buckles and the grass grows through;
and God bless the grass.

God bless the grass that breaks through cement.
It's green and it's tender and it's easily bent,
but after a while it lifts up its head,
for the grass is living and the stone is dead;
and God bless the grass.

—Malvina Reynolds

Creator God
you made all things
and all you made was very good.
Show us how to respect
the fragile balance of life.
Guide by your wisdom those who have power
to care for or destroy the environment,
that by the decisions they make
life may be cherished
and a good and fruitful earth
be preserved for future generations;
through Jesus Christ our Lord
Amen.

—Church of Scotland, Panel on Worship

Traffic

Dear God,
the traffic is really bad now.
We sat in the car
for an hour without moving.
The exhaust fumes were clogging
up the air so we could hardly breathe.

Lord, help us to be more sensible
about how we travel.
Give wisdom to those who are
in positions of power,
so they can do something to help.
Stop us polluting the atmosphere even more,
just because we are too lazy to think
of an alternative.

—*Carol Watson*

Inversnaid

This darksome burn, horseback brown,
his rollrock highroad roaring down,
in coop and in comb the fleece of his foam
flutes and low to the lake falls home.

A windpuff-bonnet of fáwn-fróth
turns and twindles over the broth
of a pool so pitchblack, féll-frówning,
it rounds and rounds Despair to drowning.

Degged with dew, dappled with dew
are the groins of the braes that the brook treads through,
wiry heathpacks, flitches of fearn,
and the beadbonny ash that sits over the burn.

What would the world be once bereft
of wet and wildness? Let them be left,
O let them be left, wildness and wet;
long live the weeds and the wilderness yet.

—Gerard Manley Hopkins

Collect for Rogation Day

Almighty God
whose will it is that the earth
should bear its fruits in their seasons:
direct the labour of those who work on the land
that they may employ the resources of nature to your glory
for our own well-being
and for the relief of those in need.
Through Jesus Christ our Lord
Amen

—*Church of England Alternative Service Book*

We give thanks for places of simplicity and peace. Let us find such a place within ourselves. We give thanks for places of nature's truth and freedom, of joy, inspiration and renewal, places where all creatures may find acceptance and belonging.

Let us search for these places in the world, in ourselves and in others. Let us restore them. Let us strengthen and protect them and let us create them.

May we mend this outer world according to the truth of our inner life and may our souls be shaped and nourished by nature's eternal wisdom.

—*Michael Leunig*

SACRIFICE

The coming

And God held in his hand
a small globe. Look, he said.
And the son looked. Far off,
as though through water, he saw
a scorched land of fierce
colour. The light burned
there; crusted buildings
cast their shadows; a bright
serpent, a river
uncoiled itself, radiant
with slime.
  On a bare
hill a bare tree saddened
the sky. Many people
held out their thin arms
to it, as though waiting

for a vanished April
to return to its crossed
boughs. The son watched
them. Let me go there, he said.

—R.S. Thomas

Reconciliation

Look at the stagnant water
where all the trees were felled.
Without trees, the water-holes mourn.
Without trees, the gullies form,
for the tree-roots to hold the soil –
are gone.

These friends of ours
give us shade.
They draw the rain clouds,
breathe the moisture of rain.

I, the tree ... I am your friend.
I know you want wood
for fire:
to cook your food,
to warm yourself against cold.
Use my branches ...
What I do not need
you can have.

I, the human being,
your closest friend,

have committed a serious offence.
As a *ngozi,* the vengeful spirit,
I destroyed you, our friends.
So the seedlings brought here today
are the 'bodies' of restoration,
a sacrifice to appease
the vengeful spirit.
We plant these seedlings today
as an admission of guilt
laying the *ngozi* to rest,
strengthening our bonds with you,
our tree friends of the heart.

Indeed there were forests,
abundance of rain
but in our ignorance and greed
we left the land naked.
Like a person in shame,
our country is shy
in its nakedness.

Our planting of trees today
is a sign of harmony
between us and creation.
We are reconciled with the earth
through the body and blood of Jesus
which brings peace;
he who came to save
all creation.

—*Association of African Earth-keeping Churches*

He is the image of the invisible God, the firstborn of all creation; for in him all things in heaven and on earth were created, things visible and invisible, whether thrones or dominions or rulers or powers – all things have been created through him and for him. He himself is before all things, and in him all things hold together. He is the head of the body, the church; he is the beginning, the firstborn from the dead, so that he might come to have first place in everything. For in him all the fullness of God was pleased to dwell, and through him God was pleased to reconcile to himself all things, whether on earth or in heaven, by making peace through the blood of his cross.

—*Colossians 1:15–20*

Reredos

The reredos was not
an ecclesiastical adornment
of symbols
but plain glass
with the danger
of distracting the celebrant
from
the properties of the communion table;
for
in the translucence
the green earth
budded in the morning view
the river was in bloom,
the air a joyous flight
and the sunshine

set the clouds ablaze,
and I noticed
the priest's eyes
as it were unconsciously
placing his hand
on these gifts
as though these
were
the bread and wine.

—Euros Bowen, from the Welsh

Bread prayer

As this bread was once scattered seed, O Bread of life, sown in the earth to die and rise to new life, so gather all peoples together in one humanity of your coming new age. Restore the broken life of your creation; heal the disfigured body of your world; draw all creatures into yourself through the cross and in the power of your risen life. And grant to all the faithful departed a share in your bliss, that with them we too at the end may be welcomed into your kingdom through your inexhaustible grace, and guided by your indwelling Spirit.

—Church of South India

St Kevin's house-mates

An angel of God came to St Kevin and said, 'Oh saint of God, God has sent me to you, to bring you to the place which the Lord has appointed for you, east of the smaller lough, to be with your brothers there, for that will be the place of your resurrection.'

'If it's all the same to God,' said Kevin, 'I would rather stay here, where I have laboured for Christ, till I die.'

The angel replied, 'If you go to that place with your monks, there will always be many sons of life there till the end of the age, and your monks after you will have no lack of earthly goods. And many thousands of blessed souls will rise with you from that place to the kingdom of heaven.'

'True, holy messenger,' said St Kevin. 'It is impossible for monks to live in that valley hemmed in by mountains, unless God helps them by his power.'

Then the angel replied, 'Listen to these words, man of God. If you so desire, God will feed fifty of your monks there with heavenly bread and no earthly food at all, if they remain one in spirit with Christ after you, and whenever one dies, another will take his place in the fear and love of God, in habit and profession, till the day of judgement.'

St Kevin said, 'Now I am not happy that there should be so few monks after me in that place.'

Then the angel replied, 'If you do not like there being so few, then many thousands will live there, prosperously and without poverty, God supplying their worldly needs for ever ... Indeed, if you want these four mountains which enclose the valley to be levelled into gentle fertile fields, your God will do it for you, without a doubt.'

St Kevin said, 'I do not want the creatures of God to be moved because of me. My God can help the place in some other way. And what is more, all the wild creatures on these mountains are my house-mates, familiar and gentle towards me, and they would be sad about what you have said.' And talking together like this, the angel of God and St Kevin walked to that place over the waters of the lough.

—*Anon. Irish*

THE NEXT STEP

The summer day

Who made the world?
Who made the swan, and the black bear?
Who made the grasshopper?
This grasshopper, I mean –
the one who has flung herself out of the grass,
the one who is eating sugar out of my hand,
who is moving her jaws back and forth instead of up and down –
and who is gazing around with her enormous and complicated eyes.
Now she lifts her pale forearms and thoroughly washes her face.
Now she snaps her wings open, and floats away.
I don't know exactly what a prayer is.
I do know how to pay attention, how to fall down
into the grass, how to kneel down in the grass,
how to be idle and blessed, how to stroll through the fields,
which is what I have been doing all day.

Tell me, what else should I have done?
Doesn't everything die at last, and too soon?
Tell me, what is it you plan to do
with your one wild and precious life?

—*Mary Oliver*

Open your eyes

You never enjoy the world aright, till you so love the beauty of enjoying it, that you are covetous and earnest to persuade others to enjoy it. And so perfectly to hate the abominable corruption of humans in despising it, that you had rather suffer the flames of hell than willingly be guilty of their error. There is such blindness and ingratitude, and damned folly in it. The world is a mirror of infinite beauty, yet no one sees it. It is a temple of majesty, yet no one regards it. It is a region of light and peace, did not human beings disquiet it. It is the Paradise of God. It is more to humanity since we are fallen than it was before. It is the place of angels, and the gate of Heaven. When Jacob waked out of his dream, he said, 'God is here and I wist it not. How dreadful is this place. This is none other than the house of God, and the Gate of Heaven.'

—*Thomas Traherne*

Finding a voice

It is only where a significant, vocal and active section of society which has its own frame of reference (as Christians have their sense of responsibility to God for Creation) expresses its priorities for policies, that the Government, which has the executive power, may be moved to act accordingly. This is not a simple matter, but it is not impossible either, and it is a part the Church should play. The Church itself contains many interests and diverse points of view, yet these can be held together on this issue by the affirmation that this is God's world which is valuable to Him and hence must be cared for as something with its own intrinsic value.

—*Church of Scotland Department of Ministry and Mission*

No mere flotsam and jetsam

I refuse to accept despair as the final response to the ambiguities of history. I refuse to accept the idea that the 'isness' of our present nature makes us morally incapable of reaching up for the eternal 'oughtness' that forever confronts us. I refuse to accept the idea that human beings are mere flotsam and jetsam in the river of life unable to influence the unfolding events which surround them.

—*Martin Luther King*

God help us to change

God help us to change. To change
ourselves and to change our world.
To know the need for it. To deal with
the pain of it. To feel the joy of it.
To undertake the journey without
understanding the destination.
The art of gentle revolution.
Amen.

—*Michael Leunig*

Circuit

I make my circuit
in the fellowship of my God
on the machair, in the meadow
on the cold heathery hill,
on the corner in the open,
on the chill wind dock,

to the noise of drills blasting,
to the sound of children asking.

I make my circuit
in the fellowship of my God
in the city street
or on spring-turfed hill,
in shop-floor room
or at office desk.

God has no favourite places.
There are no special things.
All are God's and all is sacred.
I tread each day
in light or dark
in the fellowship of my God.

Be the sacred Three of glory
interwoven with our lives
until the Man who walks it with us
leads us home
through death to life.

—*Kate McIlhagga*

Two Rogation Liturgies

These two liturgies are based on the old tradition of rogation days (Latin, *rogare,* to ask) when people used to walk in procession round their fields and parishes asking for God's blessing on their work. They would stop at various 'stations' along the way to pray for their crops and animals, often sprinkling them with holy water. Traditional dates for this were either 25th April (once the pre-Christian festival of Robigalia which had a similar purpose) or one of the three days leading up to Ascension Thursday. Rogation days survived the Reformation in England, but gradually fell into disuse as people moved from villages into towns and cities, and away from agriculture into other kinds of work. Very few people in the 'developed' world now live, work and worship within an area small enough to be encompassed on foot. Recently, however, some local churches have begun experimenting with the tradition, seeing it as a way of praying for the whole of creation. City people have often led the way here, as well they might, knowing at first hand the effects of pollution and environmental degradation.

The two liturgies below are offered as a contribution to this revival. Liturgy A, by Ruth Burgess, is in fact four liturgies which can be used separately or together. It is full of ideas for informal celebrations, with a particular emphasis on human work – and play! Liturgy B is more traditional in form but with a strong emphasis on care for the earth.

ROGATION LITURGY A

These prayers can be used in rural or urban areas and although they are full of suggestions, the local environment must be your starting point when planning a route. The basic concept is to walk around the parish/the local area, praying for all who work there. In rural areas it may be possible to pray for growing crops. In urban areas it might make more sense to pray outside a local food shop or stand under a tree and thank God for the spring. There may be particular factories or landmarks that you want to include.

There are four liturgies, based on the elements (water, air, fire, earth), and they can be used in any order. There are suggestions for a closing order of worship, and also for prayers for those who are not in paid work. When there are children involved in the worship a stop at a local school could be included.

The four liturgies follow a format:

> Suggestions for a meeting place
> Opening responses
> Psalm
> Prayers
> Action

There are some suggestions for songs and hymns. An accompanying band might be useful in moving from place to place. You might also want to create an elemental banner/s.

When choosing actions choose ones that are within your resources and fit in with your timing. These prayers could take all day, or an afternoon, or could be used as separate acts of worship on different days.

Local environment will focus which workers you pray for and you might choose to create a responsive prayer to enable the whole group to make a verbal response. The last suggestion for prayers in each section is based on a global justice issue ... there may be others in which you already have concerns.

Try to make your route accessible for differently-abled people and/or plan stopping-places that can be accessed by transport. The liturgies are designed to be led by a number of leaders. If you meet in an unsheltered spot you might need to think about audibility, especially when children are reading.

Each act of worship is complete in itself and any order can be used, depending on the local environment. You could finish at any of the four meeting places or you could have a closing act of worship somewhere else.

These prayers deliberately include elements of fun. Enjoy yourselves!

* * *

FIRE

Meeting place: under a street light, near a solar light, round a bonfire, near a restaurant, by a barbecue, round a brazier, in bright sunlight …

Burning in a bush
blazing in a fiery pillar
Moses met you
COME GOD AND MEET US NOW

Roasting fish in embers
sitting round a bonfire
disciples met you
COME GOD AND MEET US NOW

Fire around their heads
holiness in their lives
believers met you
COME GOD AND MEET US NOW

PS 104
Praise God, O my soul
O God, my God, how great you are.
You are covered with majesty and glory;
you cover yourself with light
you use the winds as your messengers
and flashes of lightning as your servants.
You created the moon to mark the months;
the sun knows the time to set.
You look at the earth and it trembles,
you touch the mountains and they pour out smoke.

Alternative/additional readings:
Acts 2:1–4
Exodus 3:1–5
Daniel 3

Pray for: electricians, chefs, welders, cooks, street-lamp servicers and menders, firework producers, workers on oil rigs, firefighters, candlemakers, scientists, metal workers, crematorium workers, lighters of birthday candles, ... those without warmth and shelter.

Action: light lamps, light torches, cook food, set off fireworks, make a bonfire, light sparklers, install a solar lamp.

* * *

AIR

Meeting place: airfield, playground/near a roundabout or swings, near a wind-tunnel, e.g. between two blocks of flats, on high ground.

Starmaker God
rain bringer
wind blower
BREATH OF GOD, BREATHE ON US

Storyteller God
bird watcher
hill climber
BREATH OF GOD, BREATHE ON US

Pentecostal God
fire dancer
life bringer
BREATH OF GOD, BREATHE ON US.

Ps 104
Praise God, O my Soul
O God, my God, how great you are.
You have spread out the heavens like a tent
and built your home in the heights.
You use the clouds as your chariot
and ride on the wings of the wind.
The cedars of Lebanon get plenty of rain
there the birds build their nests.
When you send out your spirit
all life is created.
You breathe new life into the earth.

Alternative/additional readings:
Ezekiel 37:1–10
John 3:5–9

Pray for: astronauts, tyremakers, wind turbine makers, aeroplane crews, helicopter pilots and rescue crews, hang-gliders, fairground workers, bee-keepers, steeplejacks, falconers … those who live in polluted environments.

Action: fly kites, blow bubbles, have a turn on a roundabout or a swing, give each other a swing (gently), climb a tower, play on an inflatable/bouncy castle, fly a flag or a banner.

* * *

EARTH

Meeting place: garden, allotment, park, graveyard, near a food shop, by grass or weeds growing through concrete, on a hill, on a footpath, in a quarry, near a building site ...

You, God, are our rock
our sure foundation
our solid ground
YOU ARE OUR STRENGTH

You, Jesus, are our bread
our death and resurrection
our common ground
YOU ARE OUR HOPE

You, Holy Spirit, are our wildness
our loving wisdom
our holy ground
YOU ARE OUR JOY

Ps 104
Praise God, my soul
O God, my God, how great you are.
You have set the earth firmly on its foundations
and it will never be moved.
You make grass for the cattle
and plants for us to use
so that we can grow our crops
and produce wine to make us happy

olive oil to make us cheerful
and bread to give us strength.

Alternative/additional readings:
Matthew13:1–9
John 12:20–26

Pray for: town-planners, builders, farmers, archaeologists, shopkeepers, gardeners, JCB drivers, mountain rescue teams, tunnellers and quarry workers, park-keepers, gravediggers, walkers, miners ... those who are hungry ...

Action: buy food, eat food, plant seeds, pick fruit or vegetables, build a cairn of stones, make sandcastles, dig a hole ...

* * *

WATER

Meeting place: fountain, sewer cover, drain, tap, river, sea, swimming pool, pond, near a brewery, a distillery, or bottled water factory, on a bridge over a stream, at a well, near puddles.

Playful God
creator of sea monsters
keeper of the shorelines
WE PRAISE YOU

Joyful God
listener at a well
healer by a pool
WE PRAISE YOU

Mysterious God
dancer at creation
mover over the deep dark waters
WE PRAISE YOU

PS 104
Praise God my soul
O God, my God, how great you are.
When you rebuked the waters they fled.
They rushed away when they heard your shout of command.
They flowed over the mountains and into the valleys
to the place you had made for them.
You set a boundary they can never pass
to keep them from covering the earth again.
The ocean is large and wide.
The ships sail on it, and in it plays Leviathan
the sea monster you made to amuse you.

Alternative/additional readings:
Jonah 1:17–2:10
Mark 4:35–41
John 5:1–8

Pray for: plumbers, engineers, vine growers, swimming baths attendants, sewerage workers, fishers, wine-makers, brewery workers, distillers, umbrella-makers, lifeboat crews, factory workers … those who have no access to fresh clean water …

Action: sprinkle each other with water, drink a local beverage, paddle in a local pond, play Pooh Sticks at a bridge, sail a model boat, stamp in puddles, wash one another's hands and/or feet.

MUSICAL RESOURCES

Many traditional songs and hymns have elemental themes and if worship is outdoors it is probably best to stick with what is familiar.

Using chants rather than hymns will eliminate the need for song sheets. The use of songs with choruses with which everyone can join in has the same advantage. Many traditional work songs are of this type.

The following songs can all be found in *Common Ground* (St Andrew Press 1998):

She sits like a bird (32)
The peace of the earth (121)
Christ be our light (21)
Glory to God above (39)
I, the Lord of sea and sky (50)
Spirit of God, come dwell within me (82)
O the life of the world (97)
Praise God for the harvest of orchard and field (102)
Sing to God with gladness, all creation (112)

The seed is Christ's (135)
We are marching in the light of God (139)

Music (use of a drum?) and songs may be played or sung when moving between meeting places.

UNEMPLOYMENT

Although the focus of rogation prayers is for people who are working, the reality of most locations is that there will be people who are not able to find work.

These two prayers are for those who are unemployed:

Remind me

In the days
when there is
no paid work

In the days
when no one is
willing to hire me

In the days
when the system
wears me down

Remind me God
you love me
and need me.

Day in, day out

Day in
day out
no money
no meaning

Day in
day out
no security
no strength

Day in
day out
no work
no warmth

Day in
day out
God breathes
God listens

Day in
day out
God loves
God loves me.

— *Ruth Burgess*

It may also be good to include space in your prayers for those who are ill and those whose caring responsibilities prevent them from taking paid work. Also for those who are prevented from working by disabling working environments.

CLOSING ACT OF WORSHIP AND CELEBRATION

If possible finish with a celebratory act that includes all four elements:
Food, drink, bouncy castle and fireworks
Picnic, barbecue, Pooh sticks and kite flying
A meal with candles, balloons, and a local beverage
Paddling, sandcastle-building, kites and sunbathing
Puddle-splashing followed by a visit to the fairground and chips

Act of worship

Ps 104
Praise God, O my soul,
O God my God,
how great you are.
God you have made so many things
how wisely you have made them all.
I will sing to God all my life.
As long as I live I will sing God's praises.
May God be pleased with my song
for my gladness comes from God.

Either sing 'The peace of the earth' (CG 121)

Or say together:

God of the elements, bless us
breathe on us
wash us clean
warm us
root us in your good ground
and nourish our living with holy joy. AMEN

ROGATION LITURGY B

Liturgies like this take careful planning, so here are a few points to think about beforehand:

Traditionally rogation days were fast days. How about holding your procession before breakfast?

Unless you are lucky enough to have a farm or garden nearby why not make a symbolic journey, with stations centred on a tree, for example, a flower bed, a display of farm produce, a feeding area for wild birds, some symbols of local industry.

It is important that most of it take place outdoors and on foot.
What role will there be for children and young people?
Do you want to make banners and/or carry a processional cross?
Would it help to have a small group leading the music?
How accessible is the route for people with special needs?

Will animals be included at any point? If not, why not? If so, how can this be managed safely and simply?

Will everyone be able to hear? Remember that voices do not carry so easily outdoors.

Can you do without hymn books and orders of service, e.g. by choosing simple chants or hymns with easy responses or antiphons?

Introduction

People should gather in the church for a *short* act of worship, e.g. morning prayer, after which the leader(s) explains what the rogation liturgy is about and what is going to happen. He or she then announces the first processional hymn and people sing a verse or two together before moving off. If the procession is led by children, someone who knows the route should accompany them.

First station

(An open place, preferably with a good view, water and earth nearby. Theme: the universe, creation.)

First reader

A reading from the book of Genesis
In the beginning God created the heaven and the earth. And the earth was without form and void: and darkness was upon the face of the deep. And the Spirit of God moved upon the face of the waters. And God said, Let there be light: and there was light. And God saw the light, that it was good: and God divided the light from the darkness. And God called the light day, and the darkness God called night. And the evening and the morning were the first day.

Response: Thanks be to God.

Worship leader

Let us pray:
God of power and mystery,
who made the universe out of nothing,
everything that exists owes its being to you
and without you there would be neither time nor space
landscape nor any companion creatures:
we thank you for the gift of life on earth:
for the ground beneath our feet and the sky above
for water and air and for the morning light.
Help us to see this world as you do, with the same loving eye.
You who live and reign for ever and ever.
Amen.

Processional hymn (while walking)

Second station:

*(Within sight of a garden, greenhouse or allotment, a farm, a field or the sea.
Theme: farming and fishing, domestic animals, pets)*

Second reader

A reading from the book of Joel (2:15–16, 21–22)
Blow the trumpet in Zion;
sanctify a fast;
call a solemn assembly;
gather the people.
Sanctify the congregation;
assemble the aged;

gather the children,
even infants at the breast.
Let the bridegroom leave his room
and the bride her canopy ...
Do not fear, O soil;
be glad and rejoice,
for the Lord has done great things.
Do not fear, you animals of the field,
for the pastures of the wilderness are green;
the tree bears its fruit,
the fig tree and vine give their full yield.

Worship leader

Let us pray:
God of our mothers and fathers in their many generations
bless those who provide us with the basic necessities of life;
farmers and gardeners, fishing communities,
transport workers and people working in the food industry.
Help us to be more aware of the needs of our brothers and sisters
both here and in other parts of the world.
Increase our respect for the inheritance of future generations
and for the plants and animals in our care.
Teach us to use wisely the things of earth, for the good of all,
you who live and reign for ever and ever.
Amen.

Processional hymn

Third station

(Within sight of trees, grasses or wild flowers, near a bird-feeder or bird-bath. Theme: wild plants and animals, birds, insects, etc.)

Third reader

A reading from the Gospel according to St Luke (12.6–7, 13–15, 22–31)
[Jesus said to them:] 'Are not sparrows sold for two pennies? Yet not one of them is forgotten in God's sight. But even the hairs of your head are all counted. Do not be afraid; you are of more value than many sparrows.' Someone in the crowd said to him: 'Teacher, tell my brother to divide the family inheritance with me.' But he said to him, 'Friend, who set me to be a judge or arbitrator over you?' And he said to them, 'Take care! Be on your guard against all kinds of greed; for one's life does not consist in the abundance of possessions ... Therefore I tell you, do not worry about your life, what you will eat, or about your body, what you will wear. For life is more than food, and the body more than clothing. Consider the ravens; they neither sow nor reap, they have neither storehouse nor barn, and yet God feeds them. Of how much more value are you than the birds. And can any of you by worrying add a single hour to your span of life? If then you are not able to do so small a thing as that, why do you worry about the rest? Consider the lilies, how they grow; they neither toil nor spin; yet I tell you solemnly, even Solomon in all his glory was not clothed like one of these. But if God so clothes the grass of the field, which is alive today and tomorrow is thrown into the oven, how much more will he clothe you – you of little faith! And do not keep striving for what you are to eat and and what you are to drink and do not keep worrying. For it is the nations of the world that strive after these things, and your Father knows that you need them. Instead strive for his kingdom and these things will be given to you as well.'

Worship leader

Let us pray:
Son of Mary, you took flesh and entered our world,
uniting yourself to the created world and all created beings.
You showed us a love without boundaries:
for friends and enemies, sparrows and ravens.
You passed through death, to raise us up in hope,
reconciling all things to yourself, in heaven and on earth.
Strengthen our trust in your providence
that we might cling to you rather than to an excess of goods
and possessions.
And teach us to seek your way for all creatures in this world,
you who live and reign for ever and ever.
Amen.

Processional hymn

Fourth station

(Back in front of the church. Theme: God's presence with creation)

Fourth reader

A reading from the Holy Gospel according to St John (16:12–15)
[Jesus said:] I still have many things to say to you, but you cannot bear
them now. When the Spirit of truth comes, he will guide you into all the
truth; for he will not speak on his own, but will speak whatever he hears,
and he will declare to you the things that are to come. He will glorify me,
because he will take what is mine and declare it to you. All that the Father
has is mine. For this reason, I said that he will take what is mine and
declare it to you.

Worship leader

Let us pray:
Holy Spirit, you hovered over the waters at the dawn of creation.
Your power was at work before ever human child was born
moving among the plants and animals in ways beyond telling.
You anointed Jesus to bring good news to the poor and hope to all peoples.
When his work on earth was completed
and he was about to return to the Father
he promised not to leave us orphans
but gave us the consolation of your presence.
Guide our hearts and minds with your light
that we may see more clearly the way that we should go
and use wisely the gifts that God has given us on earth.
We ask this in the name of Jesus the Lord
Amen.

The liturgy could end here, with a blessing and/or with a final hymn, or people could re-enter the church for a celebration of the Eucharist or a service of holy communion. Either way, there should be an opportunity for people to meet afterwards, for light refreshments, maybe even for breakfast.

References and biographical notes

Every effort has been made to trace copyright holders of all items reproduced in this book. We would be glad to hear from anyone whom we have been unable to contact. Additional acknowledgements can be found on pp.5–7.

Page 39

'Night herons', by Judith Wright, from *Collected Poems 1942–70*, published by Angus and Robertson, 1971. Reproduced by permission of HarperCollins Australia. One of Australia's greatest twentieth-century poets, Judith Wright (1915–2000) was also an environmental activist and campaigner for the rights of aboriginal peoples.

Page 40

'Bright moon, scattered stars …' from John Carden, *A Procession of Prayers*, London, 1998, 13. Adapted.

Page 41

'The bonnie broukit bairn' by Hugh MacDiarmid from *Selected Poems*, Penguin Books, Harmondsworth, 1970, 17. Used by permission of Carcanet Press. Broukit – neglected; crammasy – crimson; wheen o' blethers – pack of nonsense; haill – whole; clanjamfrie – jing-bang. Born Christopher Grieve in the Border town of Langholm in 1892, MacDiarmid was a giant of the Scottish cultural renaissance of the mid-twentieth century. He died in 1978.

Page 42

'Today' from *Glasgow Zen*, Glasgow Print Studio, 1981, 12. New expanded edition Canongate, Edinburgh 2002. Alan Spence, writer and contemplative, was born in Glasgow in 1947. He also runs the Chinmoy Meditation Centre in Edinburgh, together with his wife.

'Oh Lord our God, if you are so lovely …' Henry Suso (1295–1366) was a Dominican friar and a pupil of Meister Eckhart.

Page 43

'Sweeney's island hermitage' from *Buile Suibhne/The Frenzy of Suibhne*, ed. J.G. O'Keeffe, §45, p.96–7. Editor's translation and title. Sweeney was an imaginary king who panicked on the battlefield and was forced to live out in the wilds. Carraig Alastair is Ailsa Craig, off the coast of Ayrshire in Scotland. The 'beds' in the last stanza are rocky structures, said to have been the beds of saints.

Page 44

'Ealghol: dà shealladh'/'Elgol: two views' from *Etruscan Reader IX*, Buckfastleigh, 1999. Also in *Wish I Was Here: a Scottish multicultural anthology*, ed. Kevin MacNeil and Alec Finlay, Edinburgh, 2000, 126–7. Meg Bateman, poet, was born in Edinburgh in 1959 and lives on the Isle of Skye.

Page 45

'Paw marks' from *Civilisation and Ethics: philosophy of civilisation*, part 2, trans. C.T. Campion, second edition, A&C Black, London, 1929, 232–3. Albert Schweitzer (1875–1965) was a distinguished theologian who become a medical missionary in Africa. He is mistaken in laying the blame wholly on Descartes, who believed that animals function like machines, but allowed that they might have feelings. It was his follower, Nicholas Malebranche (1638–1715), who claimed that animals 'eat without pleasure and cry without pain'.

Page 47

'Be exalted, O God ...' from the New Revised Standard Version of the Bible (NRSV).

'Laud ye the Lord' from P. Hately Waddell, *The Psalms: frae Hebrew intil Scottis*, first published 1871, reprinted 1987, p.105, Aberdeen University Press. Lift – heaven; yirth – earth; gryfes – sea monsters; howe – deep; lowe – fire, frost; frutefu' stoks – fruit trees; brute o' the field – wild animal; wurblin' – creeping; fliean feddyr – flying feather; right-rechters – right-acting people; till – to.

Page 48

'Canticle of Creation' – editor's translation from the original Italian of *Cantico delle Creature*. St Francis of Assisi, alias Francesco Bernardone (1181/2– 1226) gave up a comfortable bourgeois inheritance for a life of prayer and poverty on the fringes of the church. He is said to have written the first part of this Canticle after a particularly tormented sleepless night.

Page 50

'Mohawk prayer' is a contemporary interpretation of traditional Hotinonshon:ni philosophy from *The United Methodist Book of Worship*, Nashville, 1992, 558. Sue Ellen Konwanerahtaién:ni Herne is an Akwesasne Mohawk. She spent eight years as parish assistant in the Hogansburg United Methodist Church and now works in the Akwesasne Museum. She is a 1982 graduate of the Rhode Island School of Design.

'Glorious Lord' is a tenth/eleventh-century hymn. Translator, Oliver Davies. From Oliver Davies and Fiona Bowie, *Celtic Christian Spirituality*, SPCK, London, 1995, 28.

Page 51

'Even the sparrow' quoted from the NRSV.

Page 52/3

'Eòsai bu chòir a mholadh'/'Jesus, worthy of praise' collected from Mary Ferguson from Obbe, Harris, by Alexander Carmichael. *Carmina Gadelica*, Edinburgh, 1900, I.14, 38–41. Editor's translation.

Page 54

'Exactly as He wishes it to be' from 'Science within Islam: learning how to care for our world', in Fazlun Khalid & Joanne O'Brien, *Islam and Ecology*, WWF/Cassell, London, 1992, 37–8. Used by permission of WWF-UK.

'Through heaven and earth and sea ...' from Apologetic Sermon 3, 'On the Holy Icons' quoted in John Chryssavgis, 'The World of the Icon and Creation: an Orthodox Perspective on Ecology and Pneumatology', in Hessel and Ruether (eds) *Christianity and Ecology*, Cambridge, 2000, 86. Leontius of Salamis in Cyprus lived during the seventh century.

Page 57

'Barley field' from *Six Poems*, School of Poets, Edinburgh, 1977. Dorcas Symms lives near Smailholm in the Scottish Borders. Many of her poems reflect her feelings for the Borders countryside and her concern for the continuity of the natural cycle.

Page 58

'Faith in a seed' from Barbara Kingsolver, *Small Wonder*, Faber & Faber Ltd, London, 2002.

Page 61

'The changes' © Kenneth C. Steven from *Iona: Poems*, Saint Andrew Press, Edinburgh, 2000, 28. Reprinted by permission of the publisher and author. Kenneth Steven (b.1968) is a poet, novelist and children's author. He was brought up in Perthshire and the Highlands continue to provide a backdrop and inspiration for his work.

Page 62

'Hear the word of the Lord ...' quoted from the NRSV.

'No longer in ignorance' from *Lay Thoughts of a Dean*, The Knickerbocker Press, London, 1926, 198–9. Inge (1860–1954) was a professor of divinity at Cambridge, a fellow of Jesus College and Dean of St Paul's in London.

Page 63

'The voice of God ' was first published in *Voices*, The Corbie Press, Montrose, 1995, 30. Brent Hodgson was born in New Zealand in 1945. He has lived in Scotland since 1970, writes fiction and poetry and believes that 'true friendship based on spiritual values is needed in the world right now!'

'A disaster' from Ted Hughes, *Crow*, Faber & Faber, London, 1972, 33. Ted Hughes was born in Yorkshire in 1930 and lived and worked mainly in Devon. He was Poet Laureate from 1984 till his death in 1998.

Page 65

'Urnaigh Iain Ruaidh'/'Red John's prayer' by Ruaraidh MacThòmais from 'Arc a' Choimhcheangail/The Ark of the Covenant' in *Creachadh na Clàrsaich/Plundering the Harp*, New Gairm Publications, Loanhead, 1982, 280–281. Ruaraidh MacThòmais/ Derick Thomson was born in Lewis in 1921. Often described as the father of modern Gaelic publishing, he is also a poet and Emeritus Professor of Celtic Studies at Glasgow University.

Page 66

'Confession' from *Common Worship 2000: Services and Prayers for the Church of England*, Church House Publishing, London, 2000, 126, copyright © The Archbishops' Council, 2000. Reproduced by permission.

Page 67

'Cry of the Earth, cry of the poor' from the book of the same title by Leonardo Boff, Orbis Books, New York, 1997, 65. Leonardo Boff is a leading figure in the Liberation Theology movement in his native Brazil and a former Franciscan priest.

Page 68

'To a mouse' from *Complete Poems and Songs of Robert Burns*, ed. James Barke, HarperCollins Glasgow, 1995, 83–4. Robert Burns (1759–96), poet and collector of traditional songs, grew up in Ayrshire where he worked on his father's farm. He later became an excise officer in Dumfriesshire. Pattle – plough-scraper; a daimen icker in a thrave – an occasional ear out of twenty-four sheaves; silly – flimsy; foggage – late grass; snell – bitter; coulter – ploughshare; but house or hald – without house or holding; thole – endure; canreuch – hoar frost; thy lane – alone; gang aft agley – often go awry.

Page 70

'Sorry' by Geraldine Murphy from *Prayers for a Fragile World*, ed. Carol Watson, Lion Publishing, London, 1991.

Page 71

'The world as it was' from *Red Rowans and Wild Honey*, Birlinn, Edinburgh, 2000, 200–1. Betsy White came from a Traveller family based mainly in Perthshire and Angus between the two world wars. The early part of her life is told in *The Yellow on the Broom*, first published by W. & R. Chambers, 1979.

Page 72

Sandra Goodwill is a poet and social worker from York. The newspaper headline refers to the twins, Kimberley and Belinda, who were brought to Britain in January 2001 after a couple in Wales paid £8,000 to a Californian Internet adoption agency. They had previously been 'sold' for $6,000 to an American couple.

Page 73

'Ojibway prayer' from *Our World, God's World*, ed. Barbara Wood, London Bible Reading Fellowship, 1986, 52. Art Solomon (1915–1998) was an elder of the Anishnabe (Ojibway) Nation in Ontario, Canada.

Page 74

'A child's pet' quoted in *The Rattlebag*, Faber & Faber, London, 1982, p.106–7. W.H. Davies (1871–1940) was born in Wales and worked his passage to and from North America several times on boats carrying live animals.

Page 75

'Let us not be in despair over human sin' adapted from Father Zosima's sermon in *The Brothers Karamazov*, Penguin, Harmondsworth, 1985, 375–6. Feodor Dostoyevsky (1821–1891) was born in Moscow and was, at various times, a soldier, convict, gambler and literary genius. Themes of sin and salvation are common in his work.

Page 77

'Our brothers, the animals' quoted in Jon Wynne-Tyson, *The Extended Circle: a Dictionary of Human Thought*, Fontwell, 1985. Adapted. Basil the Great (c.330–379) was a monk and a hermit in Syria and Egypt, and later wrote a monastic rule emphasising the common life rather than individual feats of austerity.

'God of everlasting love …' from Andrew Linzey and Tom Regan, *Compassion for Animals*, SPCK, London, 1988, 88. From an Order of Service for Animal Welfare and/or Blessing, compiled by Andrew Linzey for the Royal Society for the Prevention of Cruelty to Animals (RSPCA), 1987.

Page 78

'The hornie gollach' by Eunice Buchanan from *Scottish Poetry from MacGregor's Gathering*, selected by Jimmie MacGregor and Stephen Mulrine, BBC Books, London, 1987, 32. Eunice Buchanan, poet, lives in Lenzie. A hornie gollach is an earwig.

Page 81

Breandán Ò Madagáin is Emeritus Professor of Irish at the National University of Ireland, Galway. He has a life-long interest in nature and nature poetry in the Irish language. His books include *An Dialann Dúlra* ('The Nature Diary'), 1978, a study of an early nineteenth-century work in Irish inspired by Gilbert White.

Page 82

'From a roof in Brooklyn' from Chaim Potok, *The Book of Lights*, published by William Heinemann. Reprinted by permission of the Random House Group Ltd and Alfred A. Knopf, a division of Random House, Inc. Copyright 1981 by Chaim Potok individually and Adena Potok as trustee for Rena N. Potok, Naana S. Potok and Akiva N. Potok. Chaim Potok (b.1929) is an American rabbi, novelist and artist. This passage describes an imaginary incident from the teenage years of Gershom, an army chaplain. His parents have both died and he lives with his aunt in an apartment below.

Page 83

'The ancient wood' from the Welsh, trans. by Tony Conran in *The Peacemakers*, Gomer Press, Llandysul, 1997, 60–61. Waldo Williams (1904–71) was a Quaker, a pacifist and a Welsh-language poet.

Page 84

'God's grandeur' from *The Poetical Works of Gerard Manley Hopkins*, Norman Mackenzie (ed.), Oxford, 1990, p.139. Gerard Manley Hopkins (1844–89) was a poet and a Jesuit priest.

Page 85

'The light trap' from John Burnside, *The Light Trap*, Jonathan Cape, London, 2002, 23. Reprinted by permission of The Random House Group Ltd. John Burnside, poet and novelist, was born in 1955 and lives in Fife. According to a Church of Scotland report, in 1986 Scotland had '2500 species of native higher plants and ferns, 1300 lichens, 900 mosses and liverworts, 70 mammals, reptiles and amphibians, 150 breeding birds and 100 or more regular visitors and over 20,000 species of insects and other invertebrates.' *While the Earth Endures*, Edinburgh, 1986, 41.

Page 86

'Rainbow' by kind permission of John Agard, c/o Caroline Sheldon Literary Agency, from *Limbo Dancer in Dark Glasses*, published by John Agard in 1983. ISBN 0951046705. John Agard is a performer-poet based in England. He was born in Guyana in 1949.

Page 87

'Masai fire blessing' quoted in *Earth Prayers from Around the World*, ed. Elizabeth Roberts and Ålias Amidon, HarperSanFrancisco, 1991, 158. Source not found.

Page 88

'O God, whenever I listen to the voice ...' from Charles Upton, 'Doorkeeper of the Heart: Versions of Rabi'á' quoted in *The Green Book of Poetry*, ed. Ivo Mosely, Frontier Press,

Kirkstead, 1994, 93,4. Rabi'a al-Adawiyya (b.717–801) is a Sufi saint from Basra in what is now Iraq. In old age, she moved to Jerusalem and is buried near the church of the Ascension on the Mount of Olives.

'Miracle enough' from *Be Still and Know*, Pax Christi & The Fellowship of Reconciliation, London, 1987, 7. Pax Christi, St Joseph's, Watford Way, London NW4. Thich Nat Hanh is a Buddhist monk, originally from Vietnam.

Page 89

'West African harvest thanksgiving' from *With All God's People: Orders of Service*, World Council of Churches, WCC Publications, Geneva, Switzerland, 1989, 68.

Page 90

Neil Paynter is a writer and editor. Previously, he worked in the social work field, and on the resident staff of the Iona Community.

Page 91

'Augustine on the beauty of Creation' from *Concerning the City of God*, trans. © Henry Bettenson 1972. Published by Penguin, Harmondsworth, 1972, XXII, 24, 1075. Augustine (354–430) was bishop of Hippo in North Africa and one of the first great theologians of the Western church.

Page 95

'Everything that has the breath of life' quoted from the NRSV.

Page 96

'No absolute dominion' from encyclical letter, *Sollicitudo rei socialis/Concern for social issues*, 1987, Catholic Truth Society, London, 1988.

'The covenant with Noah' quoted from NRSV.

Page 97

'Limits to self-interest' and 'Balaam's donkey' quoted from NRSV.

Page 99

'Solomon' quoted from NRSV.

'Other lives' quoted from NRSV. Chapters 38 and 39 of Job are full of similar material, too much to quote in full. God is confronting Job with his smallness and ignorance about the workings of non-human nature, and reminding him that God has his own direct relationship with the rest of nature, including wild birds and animals.

Page 100/101

'An eilid'/'The hind' from Alexander Carmichael, *Carmina Gadelica* II.187. The Gaelic word 'seile', here translated as 'placenta', refers to something slippery and can also mean 'saliva' or 'issue'.

Page 102

'The sacrifice of thanksgiving' quoted from NRSV.

Page 103

'Elijah' quoted from NRSV.

Page 104

'Again I saw all the oppressions ...' quoted from NRSV.

'Columba and Molua's knife': Adomnán (c.628–704) was ninth abbot of Iona. This passage comes from his *Life of St Columba* (II.30). His 'Law of the Innocents' (697) was designed to protect clergy, women and children from acts of violence. Editor's translation.

Page 105

'The wolf, the lamb and the holy one of God' quoted from NRSV.

'The river of the water of life' quoted from *Good News Bible*. The water may stand for the Law or for the Wisdom of God, as sources of life and healing. Ezekiel was one of the Jewish exiles who lived in Babylon after the capture of Jerusalem in 586 BC.

Page 106

'The Word was made flesh' quoted from NRSV.

Page 107

'God in all things, all things in God' from *Athanasius: Contra Gentes and De Incarnatione*, ed. and trans. Robert W. Thompson, Oxford Early Christian Texts, 1971, 111–19. Reprinted by permission of Oxford University Press. Athanasius (c.296–373) was bishop of Alexandria and a powerful advocate for the view that Jesus (here called the Word of God) was the divine embodiment of God's life-giving creativity.

Page 108

'Temptations' quoted from NRSV.

Page 109

'Consider the lilies' quoted from NRSV.

Page 110

'The communion of goods' from 'Commentary on the Gospel of St Luke', quoted in *The Call of Creation*, The Catholic Bishops' Conference of England and Wales, London, 2002, 4.

'Hope for Creation' quoted from *Good News Bible*.

Page 111

'Being in God': St Paul speaking to the Athenians, quoted from NRSV.

'All the world arose with him' based on *In Tenga Bithnua/The Evernew Tongue*, ed. Whitley Stokes, *Eriu* 2, 98–9, §11–13. Probably tenth-century, based on Greek or Latin sources.

Page 112

'Will animals be immortal?' from *Calvin's Commentaries: The Epistles of Paul the Apostle to the Romans and to the Thessalonians*, ed. D.W. Torrance and T.F. Torrance, trans. Ross Mackenzie, Paternoster Press, London and Edinburgh, 1961, 173–4. US and Canadian rights held by Wm. B. Eerdmans Publishing Co. Commentary on Romans 8.21. Scripture quotation from the Good News Bible. Edited for inclusive language. John Calvin (1509–64) was a French lawyer and theologian and leader of the Reformation in Geneva.

Page 115/16

'Ag iasgach a' mhic-meanmna'/'Fishing the imagination' from *One Road*, Fountain Publishing, Isle of Skye, 1994, 114–5. Angus Peter Campbell is a poet and journalist. Born in South Uist, he now lives and works on Skye.

Page 116

'Patrick and the daughters of Loguire' from Tírechán's memoir on St Patrick, 26, §1–13, editor's translation, from Latin. *The Patrician Texts in the Book of Armagh*, ed. Ludwig Bieler, Dublin, 1979, 142–4. Tírechán was a seventh-century Irish bishop who collected and shaped local traditions about St Patrick.

Page 118

'Beware, soul brother' from *Beware, Soul Brother and Other Poems*, first published Nwamife Publishers Ltd., Enugu, Nigeria, 1971. Achebe (b.1930) is a poet and novelist from Ogidi in Nigeria. His *Things Fall Apart* (1958) was one of the first English-language novels to describe the encounter with Christianity and colonialism from an African perspective.

Page 120

'Lost' from *Wish I Was Here*, ed. K. MacNeill & A. Finlay, Morning Star Publications, Polygon, The Travelling Gallery and National Galleries of Scotland, Edinburgh, 2000, 23.

Hamid Shami was born in Pakistan and brought up in Glasgow where he still lives. He is a frequent contributor to the multicultural newspaper *Scotland's Oracle*.

Page 121

Lucy Menezies (b.1963) is a teacher. She lives and works in London.

Page 122

'The treatment of the earth by man ...' quoted by Jonathon Porritt in *The Green Fuse*, ed. John Button, Quartet Books, London, 1990, 149. William Temple (1881–1944) was Archbishop of Canterbury from 1942–44.

Page 123

'Disconnected souls' from Kathleen Raine, 'Outer world as inner world', in *The Green Fuse*, ed. Button (op. cit.), 178. Kathleen Raine (b.1908) is a poet, scholar and co-founder of the Temenos Academy. She lives in London.

'You haven't a hope unless ...' from 'Let the Green Spirit Live', in *The Green Fuse*, ed. Button (op. cit.), 140–1. 'Bishop Peter' is Peter Ball, former Bishop of Lewes. Jonathon Porritt (b.1950) is director of Forum for the Future and has also been co-chairman of the Green Party and director of Friends of the Earth.

Page 125

'Melangell's sanctuary' from 'Life of Melangell', translated by Oliver Davies. From *Celtic Spirituality*, ed. Davies, Paulist Press, Mahwah, 1999, 221–2. Classics of Western Spirituality. Melangell was a seventh-century Irish woman who settled in Wales. Her church was a place of pilgrimage for almost a thousand years and in 1992 was restored and reopened as a centre for people with cancer and other life-threatening illnesses.

Page 127

'Outrageous demands' from *Super, Natural Christians: how we should love nature*, SCM, London, 1997, 40–1. Abridged. Sallie McFague is Emerita Professor of Theology, Vanderbilt Divinity School and Distinguished Theologian in Residence at the Vancouver School of Theology.

'Gliocas a lorg'/'Finding wisdom' by Fearghas MacFhionnlaigh, from 'Iolair, Brù-Dhearg, Giuthas' ('Eagle, Robin, Pine'), translated by Ronald Black, in *An Tuil*, Polygon, Edinburgh, 1999, 638–9. Fearghas MacFhionnlaigh teaches art at Inverness Royal Academy. He was born in the Vale of Leven in 1948.

Page 128/29

'Casan Sioda'/'Silk Feet' from *Collected Poems and Songs of George Campbell Hay/Deòrsa*

MacIain Dheòrsa, ed. Michael Byrne, Vol. 1, Edinburgh University Press, 2000, 78–9. Used by permission of the Lorimer Trust and Estate of George Campbell Hay. George Campbell Hay (1915–84) was brought up near Tarbert, Loch Fyne, served in the Mediterranean during the war and spent most of the rest of his life in Edinburgh. He wrote poetry in several languages including Gaelic and Scots.

Page 130

Isaac the Syrian (died c.700), bishop of Nineveh, wrote only in Syriac but was translated into Arabic, Ethiopic and Greek. Vladimir Lossky (1904–58) was a Russian Orthodox theologian who worked mainly in Paris. From *The Mystical Theology of the Eastern Church*, ed. The Fellowship of St Alban and St Sergius, 3rd ed., James Clarke & Co., Cambridge, 1973, 111. Edited for inclusive language.

Page 131

'Love is ...' from 'The Sublime and the Good,' *Chicago Review* 13, Autumn 1959, 51. Iris Murdoch (1919–1999) was a philosopher and novelist.

Page 132

'What the butcher said' from *The First Step: Recollections and Essays*, ed. Aylmer Maude, 4th ed., Oxford University Press, 1961, 123–35. Tolstoy (1828–1910) is best remembered as the author of *War and Peace* and *Anna Karenina*, but he also developed his own religious and moral code, bringing him into conflict with the Orthodox church at the time and with members of his own family.

'Cruel nature and reverence for life' from Albert Schweitzer, *Reverence for Life*, trans. Reginald H. Fuller, SPCK, London, 1970, 120–122. Copyright © 1969 by Rhena Eckert-Schweitzer. Reprinted by permission of HarperCollins Publishers Inc. Edited for inclusive language. For Schweitzer, see note for p.45 above.

Page 134

'Yes to the Earth' from *Si alla Terra*, 1935, translated in *The Green Book of Poetry*, ed. Ivo Mosely, Frontier Press, Kirkstead, 1994, 11. Sibilla Aleramo alias Rina Faccio (1876–1960) was an Italian writer, feminist and social activist.

Page 135

'Antiphon for the Holy Spirit': Hildegard (1098–1179) was a Benedictine abbess and mystic from Rhinehessen in Germany. She wrote works on natural history and medicine as well as songs and visionary literature. Translated by Oliver Davies from *Saint Hildegard of Bingen: Symphonia*, ed. Barbara Newman, London, 1988; Fiona Bowie and Oliver Davies, *Hildegard of Bingen: an anthology*, SPCK, London, 1990, 118.

Page 136

'The Heaven of Animals' from *Drowning with Others* © 1962 by James Dickey and reprinted by permission of Wesleyan University Press. All rights reserved. James Dickey (1923–97) was an American poet and novelist.

Page 138

'The bells of heaven' from *Poems*, London, 1917. Ralph Hodgson (1871–1962) published his first poems in England. In 1924 he moved to Japan where he married an American missionary, Aurelia Bolliger. They later settled in Ohio.

'An elegant simplicity' from 'Thought for the Day', BBC Radio 4, 19 March 2002. Abridged. Satish Kumar is editor of *Resurgence* magazine and Director of Programme at Schumacher College, Devon. Born in India, his early influences include Jain monasticism and Gandhian religious philosophy.

Page 139

'Columbanus and the bear' from *Life of St Columban* by the monk Jonas, ed. Dana Carleton Munro, Llanerch Publishers, Felinfach, 1993, first published by University of Pennsylvania, Philadelphia, 1895, 93, §55. Columbanus or Columban was a sixth-century Irish monk who went into voluntary exile in France, Germany and Northern Italy. One of his foundations there was at Bobbio where Jonas wrote his *Life*.

Page 140

'Cheetah, antelope, hunter' from Ruth Page, *God and the Web of Creation*, SCM, London, 1996, 152–3. Ruth Page was born in Dundee and lived in New Zealand for many years before returning to Scotland in 1979 to teach theology. She was Principal of New College, Edinburgh, from 1996–9

'Creation and evolution' from Charles Darwin, The Origin of Species, Penguin Books, Harmondsworth, 1982, 459-60. First published 1859.

Page 142

'Word made flesh' © Kathleen Raine from *The Pythoness* (1949), reprinted in *The Collected Poems of Kathleen Raine* (Golgonooza Press, 2000). For biographical information see note for p.123 above.

Page 143

'Not just for us' from Hugh Montefiore (ed), *Man and Nature*, Collins, London, 1975, 67–8. Report by Anglican bishops, commissioned by the Archbishop of Canterbury, Michael Ramsey, 1971. Edited for inclusive language.

Page 144

'A community of creatures' quoted from NRSV.

'Here on the white beach ...' from 'In the Sea and Pine Country', in *The Bird Path*, Mainstream Publishing, Edinburgh, 1989, 103. Kenneth White made his name as a poet in France where he taught poetry at the Sorbonne. His 'geopoetics' is rich in natural imagery and often draws inspiration from Japan, Scotland and the Celtic saints.

Page 147

'Call to stillness' from *Worship Resources*, ed. Juanita J. Helphrey. Council for American Indian Ministries, United Church of Christ, Minneapolis. Adapted from a Dakota source, pre-1890.

Page 148

'The bodhisattva': Shantideva was a Buddhist monk and poet from eighth-century India. Stephen Batchelor (trans.) *A Guide to the Bodhisattva's Way of Life*, Dharamsala, Library of Tibetan Works and Archives, 1979, 193.

'For frightened animals' quoted in *Earth Prayers*, ed. Roberts and Amidon, New York, 1991, 254. Source not found.

Page 149

'My God, through the boldness of your Revelation ...' from *Hymne de l'Univers*, Paris, 1961, 24. Editor's translation. Born in France in 1881, Pierre Teilhard de Chardin was a Jesuit theologian and palaeontologist. He worked in China for many years where he developed a theology of a universe evolving towards God, pervaded by the creative energy of Christ holding everything together in love.

'A Border shepherd prays for a thaw' from James Hogg, *The Shepherd's Calendar*, William Blackwood, Edinburgh, 1829, vol.2, 202–3. Hogg attributes this to Adam Scott, a man famed for the boldness of his prayers and for his knowledge of the Bible. Both Hogg and Scott were shepherds in the Ettrick valley in the Scottish Borders. Hogg (1770–1835) was also a poet and a novelist, author of *Confessions of a Justified Sinner*.

Page 150

'May 6th, 1948. Ascension' from *The Sign of Jonas*, Sheldon Press, London, 1976, 103. Thomas Merton (1915–68) was a Cistercian writer and poet. Brought up in France, England and the United States, he became a monk in the Abbey of Gethsemane near Louisville, Kentucky. He and Fr Macarius seem to be celebrating a simplified Rogation Day procession.

'For the necessities of life' based on a Coptic liturgy in *In Spirit and in Truth: a Worship Book*, World Council of Churches, seventh assembly, 1991, no.10. Editor's translation.

Page 152

'A dog's prayer' from *Prières dans l'Arche,* sixth edition, Éditions du Cloître, Jouques, 1993, 29. Editor's translation. Carmen Bernos de Gasztold (1919–95) wrote her first poems while working in a stocking factory near Paris during the Nazi occupation. Never entirely at ease with the world after the war, she went to live with the Benedictine sisters at Limon-par-Igny, south of Paris, and later in Provence.

Page 153

'Animals' by Christopher Thomaidis from *Prayers for a Fragile World*, ed. Carol Watson, Lion Publishing, London, 1991.

Page 154/5

'Beannachd iasgaich'/'Fishing blessing' from Alexander Carmichael, *Carmina Gadelica*, I.117, collected from Aonghas Mac'Ill Innein, Benbecula. This prayer is said to have been used by the young men of Uist before setting out to fish on Christmas morning. Editor's translation.

Page 156/7

'Bean an iasgair'/'The fisherman's wife' from *Collected Poems and Songs of George Campbell Hay/Deòrsa MacIain Dheòrsa*, ed. Michael Byrne, Vol. 1, Edinburgh University Press, 2000, 156. Used by permission of the Lorimer Trust and Estate of George Campbell Hay. For biographical information, see note for pp.128–9.

Page 158

'The other' originally published in R.S. Thomas, *Destinations*, Celandine Press, Shipston, 1985. Used by permission. R.S.Thomas (1930–2000) was born in Wales and lived there most of his life. He was a poet and an Anglican priest.

Page 159

'War' by Josephine Davies from *Prayers for a Fragile World*, ed. Carol Watson, Lion Publishing, London, 1991.

'Women's tree-planting prayer' from a tree-planting Eucharist of the Association of African Earth-keeping Churches, ed by Inus Daneel. See M.L. Daneel, *African Earthkeepers*, vol.2, Unisa Press, Pretoria, 2000. ZIRCONN is the Zimbabwe Institute of Religious Research and Ecological Conservation. Mwari is a traditional name for the Creator.

Page 160

'God bless the grass', words and music by Malvina Reynolds © 1964 Schroder Music Co.

(ASCAP). Renewed 1992. Used by permission. All rights reserved. Malvina Reynolds was born in California in 1900 to Jewish immigrant parents. Her songs were recorded by Pete Seeger, Judy Collins, Joan Baez, the Seekers and others. She died in 1978.

'Creator God ...' from *Book of Common Order of the Church of Scotland,* Saint Andrew Press, Edinburgh, 1996, 483. Used by permission of the Church of Scotland Panel on Worship.

Page 161

'Traffic' from *Prayers for a Fragile World*, ed. Carol Watson, Lion Publishing, London, 1991.

Page 162

'Inversnaid' from *The Poetical Works of Gerard Manley Hopkins* (op. cit.), p.167. See note for p.84.

Page 163

'Collect for Rogation Day' from *The Alternative Service Book, 1980,* copyright © The Central Board of Finance of the Church of England, 1980; The Archbishops' Council, 1999. Reproduced by permission.

'We give thanks for places of simplicity and peace ...' from Michael Leunig, *A Common Prayer*, Lion Publishing, Oxford, 1997. Michael Leunig is an Australian cartoonist, poet and social commentator.

Page 165

'The coming' originally published in R.S. Thomas, *Experimenting With an Amen*, Macmillan, London, 1986. Used by permission.

Page 166

'Reconciliation' by Bishop Marimba, from a liturgy for a tree-planting Eucharist, collected by Inus Daneel in M.L. Daneel, *African Earthkeepers*, vol.2, Unisa Press, Pretoria, 2000.

Page 168

'He is the image of the invisible God' quoted from NRSV.

'Reredos' from Euros Bowen, *Poems*, Gomer Press, Llandysul, 1974. Author's own translation. Used by permission of Gomer Press. For the Welsh, see *Detholion*, Cardiff, 1984, 199. Euros Bowen (1904–88) was an Anglican priest, born in the Rhondda Valley in South Wales. A reredos is a decorated panel behind an altar, usually against a wall.

Page 169

'Bread prayer' from *Worship in an Indian Context*, ed. Eric J. Lott, United Theological College, Bangalore, 1986. This is an early draft of a liturgy later authorised and modified by the Church of South India as an Alternative Liturgy.

Page 170

'St Kevin's housemates' from the Latin *Life of St Kevin in Vitae Sanctorum Hiberniae*, ed. Charles Plummer, Oxford, 1910, I. 245–6. Seventh/eighth century(?). Editor's translation.

Page 173

'The summer day' from *The House of Light* © 1990 Mary Oliver. Reprinted by permission of Beacon Press, Boston. Mary Oliver (b. 1935) is a poet and a winner of the Pulitzer prize. She lives in Massachusetts and Vermont.

Page 174

'Open your eyes' from 'Centuries of Meditations' in *Selected Poems and Prose*, ed. Alan Bradford, Penguin Books, London, 1991, 198. Edited for inclusive language. Thomas Traherne (1637–71) was a shoemaker's son from Hereford. He became an Anglican priest, but his mystical theology lay largely unpublished till the twentieth century.

Page 175

'Finding a voice' from Ruth Page, *While the Earth Endures: a Report on the Theological and Ethical Considerations of Responsible Land-Use in Scotland*, SRT Project, Edinburgh, 1986, p.15.

'No mere flotsam and jetsam' from Nobel Prize Acceptance Speech of Martin Luther King, 1964. Edited for inclusive language. Martin Luther King (b. 1929) was a Baptist theologian, preacher and leading figure in the civil rights movement which claimed voting rights for African Americans and an end to segregation. He was assassinated in 1968.

Page 176

'God help us to change' from Michael Leunig, *A Common Prayer*, Lion Publishing, Oxford, 1997. For biographical information see note to p.163.

'Circuit' from *The Pattern of Our Days*, ed. Kathy Galloway, Wild Goose Publications, Glasgow, 1996, 132–3. Kate McIllhagga was a minister of the United Reformed Church and a member of the Iona Community. She died in 2002.

Page 180

'Rogation liturgy A': Ruth Burgess is a member of the Iona Community who writes blessings, prayers and liturgies and conducts workshops to help others develop their skills in these areas. The prayers 'Remind me' and 'Day in, day out' on pp. 189 and 190 were first published in *Praying for the Dawn*, ed. Ruth Burgess and Kathy Galloway, Wild Goose Publications, Glasgow, 2000.

INDEX OF TITLES

INDEX OF FIRST LINES

INDEX OF AUTHORS

ALSO BY MARY LOW FROM WILD GOOSE PUBLICATIONS ...

St Cuthbert's Way: A Pilgrims' Companion

St Cuthbert's Way runs from Melrose in the Scottish Borders to Lindisfarne, Holy Island, off the coast of Northumberland. This book, designed as a Pilgrims' Companion, presents

- Information essential for walking the Way
- A field guide to places of interest along the route
- An introduction to St Cuthbert and his world
- Songs, meditations and stories
- Ideas and resources for a contemporary pilgrimage experience.

It will appeal to anyone with an interest in outdoor spirituality, early Celtic and Anglo-Saxon Christianity, general history and the environment, while leaving readers free to discover the meaning of their own journey. Perfect for the armchair traveller as well as those who actually walk the Way.

"What Mary Low's book does is to give a rich context for one specific pilgrimage, and in a way accessible to pilgrims of all faiths and those beyond faith. She connects St Cuthbert's Way pilgrimage with the searching and yearning common to all humanity."

— Mary Grey, editor of *Ecotheology* magazine

"Here is a chance to walk with many people of history in a land of beauty touched by the Eternal."

— David Adam

ISBN 1 901557 22 7 • 192 pp • £9.99 • Published 1999

Wild Goose Publications, the publishing house of the Iona Community established in the Celtic Christian tradition of St Columba, produces books, tapes and CDs on:

- holistic spirituality
- social justice
- political and peace issues
- healing
- innovative approaches to worship
- song in worship, including the work of the Wild Goose Resource Group
- material for meditation and reflection

If you would like to find out more about our books,
tapes and CDs, contact us at:

Wild Goose Publications
Fourth Floor, Savoy House
140 Sauchiehall Street,
Glasgow G2 3DH, UK

Tel. +44 (0)141 332 6292
Fax +44 (0)141 332 1090
e-mail: admin@ionabooks.com

or visit our website at
www.ionabooks.com
for details of all our products and online sales